STAR PERFORMANCE

*The Story of the World's
Great Ballerinas*

STAR PERFORMANCE

The Story of the World's Great Ballerinas

by WALTER TERRY

illustrated by Marta Becket

Doubleday & Company, Inc., Garden City, New York, 1954

Library of Congress Catalog Card Number: 54–5179

ACKNOWLEDGMENTS

To Lillian Moore, dancer and distinguished dance historian, for invaluable help in matters of research and for her stimulating suggestions; to Anatole Chujoy, editor of *Dance News*, for his advice on the chapter dealing with Russian ballerinas; to Genevieve Oswald, curator of the dance archives of the New York Public Library, Fifth Avenue and Forty-second Street, for her labors and her patience (both accomplished smilingly) in supplying many of the materials of research essential to this book; to Ralph McWilliams, dancer, for several delightful performance anecdotes; and to the contemporary ballet artists themselves for telling me of their experiences, their ideas, their ideals, their dreams.

To Aunt Katherine

CONTENTS

STAR PERFORMANCE

The Story of the World's Great Ballerinas

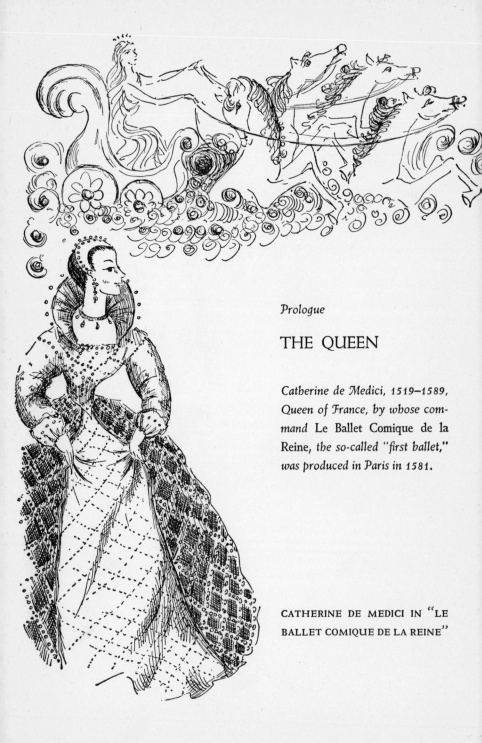

Prologue

THE QUEEN

Catherine de Medici, 1519–1589, Queen of France, by whose command Le Ballet Comique de la Reine, *the so-called "first ballet," was produced in Paris in 1581.*

CATHERINE DE MEDICI IN "LE BALLET COMIQUE DE LA REINE"

Her Majesty was an expert dancer. Not only had she ordered the creation of history's first ballet but she had also taken part in it.

The year was 1581 and the great hall of the palace was packed with some ten thousand persons, nobles of France, envoys from foreign lands, individuals of importance. Under a canopy at one end of the hall sat the royal family, and around the walls, on floor level and in balconies, the audience was seated. The center of the great room was reserved for the performers of *Le Ballet Comique de la Reine.*

Catherine de Medici, Queen-Mother of France, had brought from her native Italy a love of dancing, of pageant, of spectacle, but the culmination of those court presentations which she fostered came with *Le Ballet Comique de la Reine,* for here the diverse ingredients of masquerade, mummery, dancing, declamation, and music were united in a single creation with a single theme. Here, for the first time, was an integrated theater piece which stressed, in the words of its choreographer, "a geometric arrangement of numerous people dancing together under a diverse harmony of many instruments." True, it had its poetry, its singing, and its processionals. It relied also upon spectacular effects, such as fountains, elaborate floats, and the air-borne ascents and descents (made possible by lifting machines) of brilliantly dressed mythological figures. But the story itself—the myth of Circe the enchantress—was most certainly knit together by dancing.

More than three million francs went into the mounting of *Le Ballet Comique de la Reine.* It lasted for almost six hours, and during its course the glittering audience beheld the Queen and noblewomen as Naiads posed on the golden steps of a fountain; Circe rushing in anger from her magic garden; the gorgeous entries

14

of Mercury, Satyrs, Dryads, and others; a goddess whose chariot was led by a serpent; golden cars drawn by sea horses; Jupiter descending from heaven; and still further miracles of theatrical purpose devised by the ballet's designer, Beaujoyeulx.

Not only France but also the rest of Europe (Catherine had seen to that) knew about the splendor of *Le Ballet Comique de la Reine*, and it became something of a model for subsequent productions and for opera and true ballet of the future. But this is history in terms of form, of choreography. What of the performers and their dance aptitudes, their styles, their etiquette?

The Queen herself was a dancer who would not even permit a period of mourning to interfere with her pleasure. She participated in many court ballets along with her ladies, and we are told that their dainty actions and twinkling feet caused delight among the courtiers. And because the art of ballet at its start was guided by a Queen and her noblewomen, it followed that courtly behavior influenced the new art. Goddess-like characters from mythology, celebrated figures from history, or the choicest of virtues (in allegory) provided suitable roles for royalty, and the gracious curtsies of the court, deportment of a refined nature, and aristocratic bearing colored with royal purple the actions of dance.

Catherine de Medici, her colleagues, and her royal successors set a model which the professional ballerina inherited without question. For today, is not the ballerina still a queen, still regal in those roles which are a challenge to her stature as an artist, still aristocratic even in pure, storyless classical dancing?

Three hundred and more years have passed since *Le Ballet Comique de la Reine* was produced, yet we have not escaped the influence of the queen. Today, the young ballerina awaits with

15

fearful eagerness her first enactment of a later queen, the Queen of the Swans in *Swan Lake*. Here is her test, for it has become an almost unwritten law that she must succeed in this if she is to win her place as a ballerina. It matters little that she may be an effervescent soubrette, a superb actress-dancer in contemporary ballets, a gentle lyricist, a smiling virtuoso. She may be a success in her given area and she may wisely accent those parts for which she is best suited, but somewhere, somehow, sometime, she will wish to (or feel she must) dance the Swan Queen or an equivalent classical role.

There is more, of course, to the Swan Queen than regality, but if this element is missing, the ballerina fails. She may be and must be an assured technician and a knowing stylist, a desirable woman and a bird-like creature of magic. But she must also be a queen in command of the drama, of herself, and of the stage.

A few years ago, one of our loveliest young ballerinas completed a performance of *Aurora's Wedding* in which she played the part of the Princess. It was a good performance, too, technically brilliant, stylish but a trifle tense. Later, backstage, a senior ballerina ran up to the young star. "You frowned during your variation," she said. The junior artist suggested that multiple pirouettes, unsupported, were not always easy. "Nothing," replied the great ballerina, "is difficult for a princess. If you can't do four pirouettes without frowning, do three or two or one or stand still, but be a princess." And hours later, in the deserted theater, the senior was still coaching her junior in the behavior of royalty on stage. . . . Catherine de Medici, long dead, must have nodded (graciously, of course) her approval.

"LA PREMIÈRE
DES PREMIÈRES
DANSEUSES"

Mlle. Lafontaine, 1665?–1738, first professional female ballet dancer, made her debut at the Paris Opéra on May 16, 1681, in "Le Triomphe de l'Amour" and was hailed as the first "Queen of the Dance." Retired to a convent in 1692.

One hundred years after *Le Ballet Comique de la Reine*, the first professional female dancer, the first ballerina, made her debut in Paris in a ballet *Le Triomphe de l'Amour*. Her name was Mlle. Lafontaine and so completely did she captivate her audience that upon her was bestowed the title "Queen of the Dance."

It should be remembered that Lafontaine, celebrated as she was in her day, would hardly seem, by our standards, to be a ballerina. She knew nothing of *fouettés* or *grands jetés* or toe shoes. She wore heeled slippers, long and heavy skirts, a tight bodice, monumental wigs, and other impedimenta fashionable at the time. Her dancing, obviously, was constricted, and her dances could have been little more than polished, slightly exaggerated versions of such popular court dances as the *bourrée, sarabande,* or *passepied.*

Yet Lafontaine cannot be dismissed as a mere performer of court dances. Before her day, the ballets had been presented with casts composed of aristocratic amateurs. Royal or ducal palaces were the settings for royal and ducal performing, but with the coming of the

17

theater proper to Paris such personnel could hardly be expected to make the switch from amateur player to professional worker. Until May 16, 1681, female parts in the professional theater were taken by boys dressed as girls (all dancers were masked), but on that date Jean-Baptiste Lully (a great composer) presented four young ladies —Lafontaine, Roland, Lepeintre, Fanon—who formed the entire personnel of his dance classes, in a public performance of his own work, *Le Triomphe de l'Amour,* a royal ballet in twenty *entrées,* meaning twenty dance *divertissements,* surrounded by the spoken, sung, and acted scenes devoted to the unfolding of the theme.

There is little information available today on this woman who made—perhaps by talent and perhaps through timely fortune—history. A painting or two tell us that she was beautiful; we know how she dressed as a dancer; the range of her technique is indicated by the kinds of dances used during her period; we can discover that she made her debut in 1681 and retired slightly more than a decade later; for the rest, only tantalizing scraps of information are left to us.

There are records that the first of the first ballerinas was a very beautiful, very noble dancer. A note in a book of memoirs refers to "a certain Mlle. de la Fontaine who dances admirably" and has "charm." In those great tomes which list productions and casts of French operas, lyric tragedies, and ballets, her name is mentioned several times, but there are no descriptions of her roles or how she performed them. There is, however, a scene of excitement in the simple chronology of changing casts. In presentations of certain theater pieces before 1681 her name is missing, then it appears for a few seasons, and finally it gives way to another name, a younger dancer, a new ballerina.

MLLE. LAFONTAINE

In *Le Triomphe* she had, of course, distinguished herself. We know nothing of the responses to her appearances in such forgotten productions as *Persée*, *Amadis*, or *Le Temple de Paix*, but we are told tersely that in *Didon* Lafontaine was applauded.

Not everyone hailed the coming of the female professional dancer. In a collection of writings of the day, an item dated 1692 (the probable date of the first ballerina's retirement) touches upon "Mlles. La Fontaine et Moreau, filles de l'Opéra." In poetic form it says, in effect, that these fortunate girls have been stopped at the brink of a precipice, that they have left the Opéra, "that school of evil, Opéra, which filches from heaven so many victims," and that the Opéra has lost, through an oath, the charming support of these girls. The oath, no doubt, refers to Lafontaine's departure from stage to church, for it is generally accepted that following her last appearances with the ballet, Lafontaine retired to a convent, where she died more than forty years later, in 1738.

Did she, one wonders, ever emerge from the convent again, not to dance but to see what had happened to the profession she brought into being? She might well have approved, with understandable reservations, the dancing of her successor, Mlle. Subligny. But what would she have said of the later Prévost and her emotion-charged performances, or of Camargo, fleet, agile, short-skirted, and, by Lafontaine's standards, unladylike? We will never know what were her feelings, if any, about the dancers who followed her and outstripped her technically.

But Lafontaine is secure in history, for in her stiff and confining dress she moves with courtly elegance, transporting aristocracy to the theater as the first ballerina, as the first professional "Queen of the Dance."

Mlle. Subligny, 1666–1736?, Lafontaine's successor as principal dancer of the Paris Opéra, enjoyed the admiration of audiences in England as well as in France.

Mlle. Subligny, the next *première danseuse* at the Opéra, fell heir to Lafontaine's roles and established herself as an artist of note in newer productions. With impressive introductions, she also traveled to London, where she danced, apparently successfully, for the English public. Subligny, however, is almost as dim a figure as her illustrious predecessor, and because she was second, and not first, as a ballerina, she is, fairly or unfairly, relegated to a minor place in history. She did, however, provide the link between Lafontaine and a dancer of considerable distinction, Françoise Prévost.

Françoise Prévost, 1680–1741, successor to Subligny and dance star of the Paris Opéra for almost thirty years, had the starring part in the first ballet-pantomime to be played in France (1708), when she mimed the final act of the Corneille drama, Horace. *Retired in 1730.*

Prévost, just as every *corps de ballet* girl hopes to do, rose from the ranks to become a star. In the lists of Opéra presentations, her name moves slowly up from the end of a line toward the beginning and, with Subligny's retirement, Prévost commences a starring career which is to last for almost thirty years. These lists also tell, with cold impartiality, the periods of domination, of rivalry, and of final eclipse. For Prévost ruled long and brilliantly but she could escape neither the passing years nor the restless, eager youngsters who would strive, with ultimate success, to wrest her public from her.

She danced, of course, the principal dance roles in the Opéra's lyric tragedies and opera-ballets. *Alceste, Thesée, Roland, Armide, Zéphyre et Flore, Les Saisons, Vénus et Adonis,* and *L'Europe Galante* were but a few of the works in which she appeared, and

FRANÇOISE PRÉVOST

the length of her career is clearly indicated in the records of performances of *Amadis* (Lafontaine had once danced in this), which report her presence in 1705, 1716, and 1727.

Mlle. Prévost was far more than an executant of standard repertory; she was, indeed, something of an innovator. In 1708, she took a starring part in the first ballet-pantomime to be played in France. The event was a fete presented by the Duchesse du Maine in Sceaux, and for the occasion Prévost and her partner, Balon (who probably gave his name to the term *ballon*, meaning elasticity in a jump), mimed the final act of Corneille's *Horace*. The whole was performed without words to symphonic music, and the response to this reviving of the noble art of mime was enthusiastic in the extreme. "They vitalized their gestures and the play of facial expression to such a degree," wrote one, "that they caused tears to flow."

In dancing, Prévost must have had a technique not very different from that of Lafontaine or Subligny. She, too, was encumbered by the heavy fashions of the day and her dance forms were still those of the court—the *passepied*, the *chaconne*, the *gigue*. That she danced them well, there can be little doubt. To her performing she brought lightness, grace, accuracy, and whatever fleetness her costumes permitted, and it was even said that "composers write *passepieds* because Mlle. Prévost dances them with such fluent elegance."

Aside from her duties as *première danseuse*, Prévost was occupied in the role of teacher. Her training tasks she accomplished almost too well, for two of her most famous pupils at the Académie Royale were Camargo and Marie Sallé, destined to succeed her and, in the case of Camargo, cause her to retire before she was quite ready.

Prévost, however, did not go down without a fight. In her pupil

Camargo she soon recognized the presence of a rival. For the new-comer's first appearance in Paris, her teacher selected (quite un-wisely, as it turned out) *Les Caractères de la Danse*, a suite of dances originally created for Prévost to demonstrate her mimetic ability and her skills in the dances of the day. It was considered an extremely difficult composition and one which customarily fright-ened the most accomplished dancers of her times. But if Prévost thought that the young Camargo would suffer defeat in such choreo-graphic toils, she was sadly mistaken. The debut was sensational and Prévost herself was almost defeated. But not quite.

The senior star, still powerful, caused her student-rival to be moved to a safer spot—the back row of the *corps*—but this action and other intrigues could not long postpone the emergence of a new star. Prévost, who, of course, continued to have her faithful fol-lowers, struggled as long as she could. Her patron, a gentleman con-cerned with her well-being as well as her artistry, came to doubt her gratitude. They quarreled and parted, and his most valuable finan-cial support was withdrawn.

In 1730, Françoise Prévost, *première danseuse* and successful teacher, retired from the stage. Eleven years of life were left to her in which to mourn bitterly a cruel fate that would permit youth to supplant her or in which to remember with pride and gratitude that composers wrote *passepieds* because she danced them "with such fluent elegance."

DANCING UPWARD

Marie Camargo, 1710–1770, Brussels-born pupil of and successor to Prévost, invented the entrechat-quatre, gave accent to movements of elevation rather than to those which merely glided across the floor, and created the shortened ballerina's skirt in order to reveal her new steps. Retired in 1751.

It was, as might have been expected, something of a scandal. That Camargo should have many devoted patrons and that she should have dared to improvise a solo on the Opéra's stage were understandable, even acceptable, events. But that she should shorten her skirt and reveal part of the calf of the leg! Well, that was quite another matter. Marie Camargo, however, did just that, and with the freedom made possible by this revolution in dress, she was able to dance more fleetly, to demonstrate her mastery of the *entrechat* and the *cabriole*, to lift the ballet—for women, at any rate—from the ground and into the air. An era of horizontal—*terre à terre*—dancing for the ballerina ended, for after Camargo she could dance vertically, up into the air, as well as across the floor.

MARIE CAMARGO

Marie-Anne Cupis de Camargo was born in Brussels. Her mother, of Spanish descent, probably bequeathed to her that complexion which her critics of a later day were to term, with derogatory intent, "swarthy." From her father, a musician and dance teacher, she must certainly have inherited her musicality and her artistic instincts. Certainly, her leanings toward dancing were made manifest at an early age, for it was said that at six months she danced to the music of her father's violin. Almost every great dancer can boast of some such legend of precociousness. So let us say that the baby Marie-Anne wiggled flatteringly to her father's music and that he then and there determined to foster his obviously talented daughter's inherent skills.

When Camargo was born, April 15, 1710, the family had come upon hard times. Her father had, and was to continue to have, difficulty in supporting his family, but little Marie-Anne embodied the promise of better days to come. By the time she was eleven, she had enchanted her father's patroness, the Princesse de Ligne, and that noble lady took the whole family under her wing. The Princesse, impressed with her protégée's extraordinary talent, sent her to Paris to study under Prévost, the very *première danseuse* who was to be eclipsed by this flashing new star.

So remarkable was Camargo's progress that within a few months she was prepared to leave Paris and to make her debut, the first of a series of debuts or first appearances in several cities, at the Opéra in her native Brussels. By the time she was fifteen, she had become dance soloist at a theater in Rouen. At this point, the family's prospects appeared glowing, for not only was Camargo launched as a young star but her brother, François, was engaged to play in the orchestra her father doubled as ballet master and musician, and other members of the family were occupied in the same enterprise.

For a time, things went well with the little opera company at Rouen, but misfortune, although temporary, was to strike. The group failed to attract a sufficient number of people to make the venture a success, and the manager, clutching whatever money was available, fled to parts unknown. Once again the family was destitute, but luckily two of the star male dancers at the Paris Opéra had seen Camargo dance in Rouen and had prevailed upon their director to bring her to Paris.

At sixteen, necessary arrangements having been accomplished, Marie Camargo made her Paris debut in *Les Caractères de la Danse* at the Opéra and one of the critics of that time reported that she was young, vivacious, and intelligent; that she was Prévost's pupil and introduced by her; that her *cabrioles* and *entrechats* were effortless; but that "her art will require to be perfected before she can court comparison with her unapproachable teacher." The critic, however, did admit that her debut at the Opéra revealed her as "one of the most brilliant dancers now before the public."

The public itself hailed her with amazement and adoration. Shoes, dresses, hats, and coiffures were named after her—"à la Camargo" —and even the ladies of the court imitated her walk, her deportment.

Following her second appearance—in the lyric tragedy *Ajax*— twenty duels were supposedly fought over her, and by the time she had danced as a Grace in *Les Amours Déguisées*, Paris was in an uproar and so was Mlle. Prévost. Camargo's removal to the last line in the ensemble on orders of Prévost must have come as something of a blow to the ambitious girl, but she had not long to wait. An impulsive, sweet revenge was to be hers.

The occasion presented itself during a performance. Dumoulin, one of the principal male dancers, for some unexplained reason (inadvertently, through sudden indisposition, or was it a plot?) failed to respond to his entrance cue. Camargo, on the spur of the moment, fled her place of banishment in the ensemble and improvised a solo to the music of Dumoulin's demon dance. Her efforts were received with unreserved enthusiasm. Prévost, though battered by the battle, was not yet prepared to admit defeat.

As Camargo's teacher, the aging ballerina refused to let her appear in a ballet being organized for the Duchesse de Bourbon. This feeble attempt—Prévost's last—failed. Blondi, a star dancer among the men, invited Camargo to become his pupil. She agreed. A variation was created for her and she danced for the Duchesse in spite of Prévost. Her success was now assured.

Perhaps Prévost and Camargo set the pattern for those ballerina battles which were to spice the dance profession and delight the gossips for centuries to come. Competition was essential to the development of art and artist; rivalry was the personal by-product which invited stars and their cliques to intrigue one against the other. Carefully loosened threads in stage costumes, glass in toe slippers, rages over top billing or casting sequences, sulks, and suits were to be the historical outgrowths of the first recorded tussle between two ballerinas.

Because jealousy grew apace with her popularity, Camargo felt it wise to find herself a patron. The first of many such gentlemen was the Comte de Melun, suspected of having attempted to kidnap her following her debut. At first, Camargo refused to accept his protestations of interest, but when his attention wandered in the direction of her younger sister, Camargo capitulated. Before long, the former innocent, now a sophisticated woman, fell violently in love with a soldier-friend of the Comte's and eloped with him. She obtained an indefinite leave of absence from the Opéra, but her lover was called to active service and subsequently killed.

This love, perhaps the only meaningful one in her whole life, was never forgotten. At her death, souvenirs—faded but treasured—of this brief romance were found among her possessions. But outwardly Camargo seemed bent on pleasure. She made peace with her disapproving father, remained on amicable terms with the Comte, returned to the Opéra, and commenced a life of gaiety. Among her several patrons were the notorious Duc de Richelieu, a young friend of his, and the Comte de Clermont (third son of King Louis XIII), for whom she retired from the stage temporarily (from 1735 until her return to the Opéra in 1741) in search of domesticity.

In her ankle-length hoop skirts and high-heeled shoes, the dashing young dancer must surely have experienced a sense of frustration. Her male colleagues were far less encumbered and, watching Blondi and Dumoulin perform or rehearse, Camargo quite rightly resented the stylish fetters which held her back. She was basically an *allegro* dancer and she wished to hasten vertically as well as horizontally, so she shortened her skirts halfway up the calf and the freedom thus achieved enabled her to display the *entrechats*, the *battus*, the jumps for which she became famous. Perhaps she did not get high into the air but she was moving in that direction. Before her, the *danseuse* scarcely moved anything but head and arms; she walked, she glided, but her steps were obscured and confined. Camargo, freed, was the first of the female dancers to perform mainly with her legs.

Quite probably, early in her career, she invented the *entrechat-quatre*, one of ballet's most exciting steps. She was the first to achieve

31

that ninety-degree turnout of the limbs for which dancers had striven since the time of *Le Ballet Comique de la Reine* and since the establishment of the classical five positions of the feet some decades after that. And because she was given to bounding steps, she created (as far as we know) the *caleçon de précaution*, a most impressive name for tight-fitting drawers which, in those emergencies attendant upon flying leaps, would spare her and her public embarrassment. From the shortened skirt the classical *tutu* ultimately evolved; from the drawers slowly developed the ballet dancer's tights; from the *entrechat* and other actions invented by Camargo emerged the virtuosity which was to spell out the decline of the male dancer and establish, for years to come, the ballerina as "Queen of the Dance."

Camargo, the vertical dancer—how high did she jump? A famous painting of the dancer shows her wearing high heels, yet it is quite likely that somewhere along the adventuresome path of her career she discarded them as she came to realize that a spring from heels pressed closely to the floor would give greater elevation to her movements. Some have written of her remarkable elevation and the impression one receives is that she was very much a creature of the air, but Casanova, the almost legendary writer-adventurer-lover, noted that Camargo "bounded like a fury, cutting *entrechats* to right and left and in all directions but scarcely rising from the ground." One may ask, then, did she or did she not have elevation? By our standards, probably no.

In spite of her fame as a doer of *entrechats* and *cabrioles*, a *pas de menuet* was, apparently, the most popular of her steps. She executed this movement from left to right and back again by the very edge of the footlights. Audiences awaited eagerly this pattern and applauded their favorite enthusiastically when she came to such passages. But a *gargouillade*—which modern students like to define as "a gargle with the feet"—she considered unsuited to her sex, and this action, whenever it appeared in choreography, she replaced with a *pas de basque.*

Her favorite steps, and those which the audience favored, were almost all fleet, light, and fluid, so it is not surprising to find that she excelled in such theatricalized court dances as the *gavotte, rigaudon, tambourin, marche,* and *loure.* These dances, many of which had their ancient origins in lively peasant forms, provided Camargo with key variations (solos, duets, trios, and the like) in the more than eighty ballets which represented her total repertory.

Philosophers and poets, nobles and ordinary citizens as well as choreographers expressed their varying opinions on the artistry of this popular star. Everyone was pretty much in agreement that she was light, strong, and supple; that her vivacity and sparkle could transform a dull ballet into a success; that the brilliance of her dancing and the air of gaiety which marked her performing could lift any audience to a pitch of excitement.

But there were disagreements about Camargo's gifts, for the perfection claimed for her by her legion of ardent followers was disputed by others. Naturally, there had to be some standard of comparison, and this was found in the dancing of Camargo's closest rival, Marie Sallé. Some of Sallé's supporters admitted that Camargo was brilliant, light of step, inimitable in style, and capable of leaping as easily as a nymph, but for their own favorite they reserved charm, gentleness of movement, novelty of action, and perfect grace.

Whom can we believe? The Camargo adherents stated flatly that she was perfectly formed and that her legs were flawless, yet Jean

33

Noverre, the greatest choreographer of that era and therefore a dance expert who should have recognized perfection when he saw it, thought that Sallé was better. He recognized and appreciated Camargo's skill but he flatly stated that nature had deprived her of everything physically desirable in a dancer. The speed of her dancing, he felt, made it difficult for the onlooker to detect the defects which he had observed and he gave her credit for using her very real talents in such a shrewd manner that her deficiencies were concealed from all but the quickest eye.

Camargo, perhaps, did conceal much, but she had, as Noverre grudgingly admits, much to reveal in the way of performing, in the individual greatness of her dancing. That she was sure of her own skills, there can be little doubt. Sallé may have been her rival in the sense that she was an equally (or almost equally) popular contemporary. They danced together only infrequently—Sallé was away from Paris much of the time—but when they did, friendliness prevailed between these two artists whose styles were so utterly different that one could hardly compare them except on the basis of personal preference. Each had her faithful followers, but during the few seasons in which they appeared together at the Paris Opéra, the battles raged in the lobbies and not behind the scenes.

Camargo was especially effective in the *tambourin*, quick and gay, and Sallé in the pastoral *musette*. When the two were joined by a Mlle. Petit in a *pas de trois* from *Hypermnestre*, it was recorded that "each shone in her sphere." La Camargo, therefore, had little reason to fear rivalry and her retirement time was hers to determine. There was no repetition of her own dislodging of the aging Prévost, for Camargo, still adored, still the "Queen" of dancing at the Paris Opéra, left the stage of her own volition March 5, 1751.

Off-stage, she had always appeared to be sad—her gay life to the contrary—and when she retired with a small pension from the government and, one would guess, the income from some rather substantial investments, she turned to a lonely, quiet life of good works. In the twenty years of life remaining, she interested herself in the plight of the poor of her neighborhood and served them as best she could; and as an old lady, she surrounded herself with dogs, stray cats, six parrots, pigeons, and canaries and, perhaps, with memories of her fabulous life in the theater and the tragically abrupt life with the soldier she truly loved.

At the last, loved by only one man instead of by many, she died in the arms of her final patron, a gentleman who had worshiped her from afar for many years and had come to her as a warm and cherished friend in the closing period of her life. To him, La Camargo was ever young, ever lovely, ever pure, and he gave her a maiden's funeral, costly as befitted a star but designed in virginal white for the innocent girl.

For a dancer, Camargo's physical estate was impressive. She left a goodly amount of cash, a library, a wine cellar, and property. But her artistic bequests were, of course, monumental. Although she was very much a personality (a ballet, an opera, an art society, and several culinary delicacies were named for her) and a highly individual performer, her contributions were thoroughly impersonal, of service to the world of dance and not merely to her own glory.

She is not remembered for any particular role. In her early days at the Opéra, she played a sailoress, a Grace, a shepherdess, a bacchante, and the like; she joined Blondi and Dumoulin in a comic *pas de trois* which, one may assume, was the smash hit of the 1729 season; in *Les Talents Lyriques*, she sang as well as danced; but of

35

the countless productions in which she participated, we have little information with respect to her characterizations. Apparently, La Camargo was not much of an actress. She was, rather, a mistress of pure dance movement. The date (1730) of her invention of the *entrechat-quatre*, a basic step to this day, is historical; the dates of her enactments of specific parts are not dwelled upon by the chronicle-writers.

La Camargo, then, left her intangible but very real riches to the dancers of all time. She left the shortened skirt, which revolutionized not only the costume but also the action of the ballerina; she left that *caleçon de précaution*, which was to become the silken tights of a later day; she left an increased vocabulary of steps; she left for others a new allegro style and the beginnings of a vertical dance technique; finally, she left a heritage of virtuosity for the ballerinas yet to be born. And each of these gifts, though personal, was not personalized. None of these gifts perished with Camargo but lived on and grew and developed in the dancing stars of later generations.

Unlike choreographers, she had no ballet masterpiece to leave to posterity; unlike the great teachers and academicians, she had no established school where others might pursue a method; unlike an actress-dancer, she had no definitive characterization of a classical role upon which students could model their own interpretations. La Camargo was a dancer, and to her profession she bequeathed a better, bigger and richer way of dance than had ever before been known.

A LADY OF VIRTUE

Marie Sallé, 1707–1756, a pupil of Prévost, a contemporary of Camargo, and a star dancer of the Paris Opéra. On February 14, 1734, in London, she produced and appeared in Pygmalion, *the first full ballet to be choreographed by a woman. Retired in 1740 but made many appearances in court presentations of ballets thereafter.*

The two Maries were not at all alike. Marie Camargo invented new steps for the ballet; Marie Sallé created ballets. Camargo was a brilliant virtuoso; Sallé was known for her remarkable grace and her dramatic expressiveness. Both revolutionized theatrical costuming, but the former shortened her skirts in order to display her new techniques and the latter altered her costumes to conform with the themes of the works in which she appeared. Camargo had many lovers; Sallé had none. And so the two Maries, though rivals at the Paris Opéra, were friendly because neither invaded the special rights of the other.

Sallé died young. She was only forty-nine, yet she had danced almost all of her life. She had been born (1707) into a theatrical family. Her father, a tumbler, was probably also the manager of a little traveling troupe and her uncle was also a manager of theatrical enterprises. It is not surprising, then, that little Marie commenced to dance as a baby and was ready, by the time she was eleven, to make her professional debut. The scene, however, was not Paris but a fair, St. Laurent's Fair, and here she appeared as a dancer in a production of a comic opera, *La Princesse Carisme.*

So successful was *La Princesse Carisme* that it was presented in Paris by royal command, but whether Sallé appeared in it or not is uncertain. She did continue to dance in fairs, both in the provinces and even in Paris, from 1718 to 1721, when, at the age of fourteen, she appeared for the first time at the Paris Opéra in *Les Fêtes Venitiennes*. Like Camargo, she became a pupil of the reigning ballerina, Mlle. Prévost, and, as in the case of Camargo, the mistress became jealous of her young and talented student. Sallé waited but her progress was delayed and so, in 1725, she signed a contract with an English producer and left for London.

With her brother as her partner, she made her first appearance in the British capital in an entr'acte of a production of *Love's Last Shift*. The manager, John Rich, had inherited the theater at Lincoln's Inn Fields from his father and had been the first to produce pantomimes in London with music, elaborate scenery, ballets, and mechanical effects. When Sallé came, he had already made his theater a rival of the historical Drury Lane and so he had been able to present the French star in a setting worthy of her theatrical heritage. But the time had not yet arrived for her innovations, and Sallé appeared in the usual *entrées* and *pas de deux*. Among her presentations during her two-year stay in London was *Les Caractères de la Danse*, a suite introduced by Prévost and later danced by Camargo. Sallé, however, switched the accent from virtuosity to expressive mime, the very pattern of action which was to bring her immortality in the chronicles of dance.

Upon her return to the Paris Opéra, where she hoped to achieve ballerina status, she was given a solo in *Les Amours des Dieux*, but thereafter, for several months, she could have been seen only in the *corps de ballet*. Was the aging, irritable Prévost responsible? Or was it a punishment for having deserted Paris for London? Whatever the reason, her banishment to the ensemble could not be made to last for long. Soon she was recognized as a rival to Camargo, her special talents invited the enthusiasm of a large public, and it was not long before she was appearing on stage in principal parts not only with Camargo but with the fading queen, Prévost.

What could it have been like, a performance involving three distinctive and distinguished stars? Did Gallic courtesy prevail, or did the three upstage one another, turn on the tricks, the smiles, and the wiles? If there was an on-stage ballerina battle, one may be reasonably sure that it was limited to gracious malice. The poets as well as the public took sides, and it would be hard to imagine that three such vivid personalities would be averse to attempting to steal the show.

Sallé's biggest problem was not, however, one ballerina or two ballerinas but the Paris Opéra itself. The organization was set in its ways and although it was forced to accept the costume and technical changes which Camargo wrought, it was not prepared to go to the lengths of reform which Sallé demanded. Back she went to London to get her own way and to make history. There, on February 14 in the year 1734, she produced and danced in *Pygmalion*.

Bored with a system of choreography based upon a series of *entrées* held loosely together by a theme, Sallé determined to permit the dramatic idea, rather than flashy steps, to govern the choreography. With *Pygmalion*, which represented the first time in history that a woman had designed the choreography for an entire ballet in which she would appear, Sallé put her theories into practice. She attempted to organize dance style, gesture, music, scenery, and costumes into an integrated whole capable of serving the dramatic idea.

Since she was to play the part of the heroine in *Pygmalion*, a revolutionary change in costume was essential if her artistic thesis was to be pursued. As Isadora Duncan and Ruth St. Denis were to do two centuries later, Sallé discarded all traditional apparel (except for her corset), which she felt encumbered her body or the idea of her ballet. The still courtly costume of the French ballerina was forgotten and Sallé, in *Pygmalion*, appeared, according to a report, "without pannier, skirt, or bodice and with her hair down; she did not wear a single ornament on her head. Apart from her corset and petticoat, she wore only a simple dress of muslin, draped about her in the manner of a Greek statue."

The ballet and Sallé's costume caused a tempest in London. In this work, the star was seen as the lovely statue carved by Pygmalion. In love with his own creation, he kissed her feet, decked her with jewels, caressed her hands. His love and faith warmed her into life, and shyly, watching him dance for her, she imitated his steps, his gestures, the ways of the living.

With Malter, of a celebrated dance family, as her partner and an ensemble of six men as Pygmalion's friends, Sallé presented a new kind of ballet which was natural and expressive. She triumphed, for Londoners, including royalty, flocked to Covent Garden to see her, to fight duels in her name, to make her England's Queen (borrowed) of the Dance. Yet she invented not one new step. Her *Pygmalion* employed the movements known at the time, but she arranged them (as George Balanchine would do centuries later) in fresh sequences and she invested them with emotional colors, with nuances of mood, with dramatic purposes.

In quick succession she created *Le Masque Nuptial* and *Bacchus et Ariadne*, and at the request of Handel she appeared as Terp-

MARIE SALLÉ IN "PYGMALION"

sichore, miming and dancing to song, in the prologue of the great composer's *Pastor Fido*. A revival of John Gay's *The Beggar's Opera*, regular ballet repertory, and dance duets (in which she accented the dramatic relationship between the man and the woman rather than physical feats) called for her presence. In the same year that witnessed the première of *Pgymalion*, a benefit was held for her and, at the close of this repeat performance of *Pygmalion*, purses crammed with gold were tossed upon the stage. Sallé, beautiful and young, the personification of grace and the mistress of expressive dance, ruled London.

Yet moods change, and suddenly, without perceptible warning, the audiences turned against her and her popularity commenced to sink. She was hissed on stage and her reign, her very brief reign in London was almost over. What caused the hisses? One can only guess. The change in the public's temper came when Sallé donned male attire for a role in *Alcine*. Perhaps, for the English, this was carrying innovation and independence too far. But London had given her an artistic freedom which Paris had not, and for this she must have been grateful.

She returned to Paris a recognized star. Prévost had retired. Camargo was on a long leave of absence, and Sallé found the Opéra officials far more willing to bow to her demands. Her first appearance was in a new ballet, *Les Indes Galantes* (most recently revived, and with great fanfare, by the Paris Opéra in 1952), and the wanderer was greeted with cheers by her countrymen.

It was said, however, that her colleagues at the Opéra detested her. The reason given was that her virtuous behavior irritated them beyond measure. All the ladies of the Opéra had their patrons. Sallé had none, so she could hardly have been regarded as a potential rival in the field of patronage. Could it have been that the ladies were not so much irritated by her virtue as by the fact that Sallé needed no patron to keep secure her position in the insecure world of the theater?

Perhaps another reason for the Opéra girls' dislike of Sallé was that she was something of a self-educated intellectual. Not only was she a choreographer with unusual theories, but she was a friend of and accepted by many of the leading poets, philosophers, and thinkers of the day. Apparently she had little time for or interest in gay parties or in those who attended them. She was concerned with her own career, with the art of ballet, and with the culture of her day.

But no matter what dancers thought of her—snobbish, stuffy, peculiar—they could not fail to recognize her genius and the importance of her contributions to the art of dancing. Upon her retirement at thirty-three from the Opéra, her immediate successors adopted many of her principles of expressive action and costuming; the great choreographer and innovator, Noverre, approved her tenets, and dancers of later decades and centuries, down to the contemporary dramatic ballerina, Nora Kaye, could thank her for initial explorations into the drama of dance movement. For Sallé was not merely a fine mime (Prévost had been one, also) but an artist who had discovered that the steps and gestures of ballet, the traditional vocabulary of Western theater dance, could be made to serve the cause of drama.

When she left the Opéra in 1740, she had been a member for only nine seasons, and a fifteen-season span was the minimum requirement for a state pension. Yet so highly was Sallé esteemed by the French royal family (it is chronicled, in fact, that she was preferred to Camargo) that the King bestowed upon her a special pension, and for the next dozen years she danced on frequent occasions at Versailles and Fontainebleau in court presentations. In one of her last appearances, she performed with a talented young man, Gaetan Vestris, then a soloist at the Opéra but soon to become one of the most celebrated male dancers in history and founder of a family which was to exert profound influences on the ballet for almost a century.

In 1752, Marie Sallé gave her last performance at court. Four years later she was dead and all but forgotten. But she had danced for the greater part of her short life. She had been successful, she had been virtuous, and, as far as anyone knows, she had been happy.

With her younger brother, who had died before her great triumph in *Pygmalion*, she had taught her concepts of dance to young pupils, and although her name might have been forgotten for a time after her death, these students, the dancers who had seen her, and the audiences who had accepted her innovations surely kept alive something of her dance creed. What, for example, did Gaetan Vestris learn from her in their one performance together? Did he absorb something of her magic and could he pass it on to his equally famous son, Auguste, and to Noverre, for whom he danced so successfully? And did Auguste, as a teacher of Fanny Ellsler, give an echo of Sallé to a ninetenth-century ballerina? We cannot know when the passage of time ended a period when a master could say to his student, "Sallé told me . . ." and another era began in which Sallé's beliefs became an unidentifiable part of the tradition of dance.

While America was still a colony and before George Washington had seen and approved of his first ballet dancer, Sallé was gone. Her virtue, her grace, her unaffectedness, her ability to be voluptuous and still retain an air of modesty, her great dramatic skill were but memories in the minds of a very few and words of record in poems and yellowing reviews. Gone, too, was the vision of a statue which came to theatrical life and, with flowing hair, a free body, and expressive actions of feet and arms and face, gave life not only to a story-symbol but to dance itself.

MADELEINE GUIMARD IN "LE PREMIER NAVIGATEUR"

A PAIR OF ROGUISH EYES

Madeleine Guimard, 1743–1816, Paris-born dancer, in 1761 made her debut with the Paris Opéra as the understudy to the reigning ballerina, Marie Allard (successor to Camargo and Sallé). The title première danseuse noble was bestowed upon her. Particularly famous for her skill at characterization, for her interpretative abilities in traditional as well as in new roles. Retired in 1789.

In song and story, poets have immortalized the beautiful eyes of real or imagined heroines. There are the "dark blue" eyes of Annie Laurie, and there are sparkling eyes, sad eyes, starry eyes. But somehow the ballerina's eyes are overlooked by those who concentrate (and usually quite rightly) upon her dance movements. Not so with Madeleine Guimard, whose "roguish eyes" captivated Parisian and London audiences during the latter half of the eighteenth century. Guimard was, as her long career proved, an accomplished dancer and a sensitive artist, but her neck, which her admirers stated was the prettiest in the world, gave extra grace to her dance poses and her roguish eyes were the windows of a vital spirit.

By the time she was fifteen, Guimard, who had been born in Paris in October, 1743, was prepared to launch her own career. Ballet studies had not been easy to arrange for this fatherless child, but somehow her mother managed to pay for lessons, and such fine talent did she reveal by the time she entered her teens that she was able, with the help of friends, to obtain a job in the *corps de ballet* of the Comédie Française.

In 1758, the year in which Guimard entered the *corps de ballet*, the dances and ballets presented at the Comédie Française were received with almost as much enthusiasm as the major productions at the Opéra. Nevertheless, by tradition, the Opéra was the goal of the ambitious young dancers of the day, and Guimard was no exception.

Three years later, supported by the fine reputation earned during her seasons at the Comédie, she joined the Paris Opéra as understudy to the reigning ballerina, Marie Allard, a gifted and popular artist somewhat overshadowed by memories and legends of her illustrious predecessors, Camargo and Sallé.

For a year Guimard waited, and then in 1762 the star injured her foot and the patient understudy made her debut at the Opéra as Terpsichore in *Les Fêtes Grecques et Romaines*. It was an enormously successful debut, and for the next three decades Madeleine Guimard was destined to rule supreme. She had highly talented colleagues, but they could never rival her popularity, never disturb her immense power, never supplant her until she was ready to retire of her own volition. As the great choreographer Noverre said, "Mlle. Guimard obtained the applause of the public from her debut to retirement."

But even as early as 1763, it was clear that Guimard was of star caliber and she was made a *première danseuse noble*. The title indicated that she excelled in the classics, yet she was actually limited in her technical equipment. Mlle. Lyonnais, one of her colleagues and a dancer noted for her execution of the *gargouillade*, probably surpassed her with respect to virtuosity, and it is likely that Allard, before she became fat (ultimately she had to retire because of weight), also outshone her as a classicist. But Guimard had more than a lovely neck and roguish eyes with which to fascinate the public. Although her steps were small and kept her on the ground rather than propelling her into the air, her interpretive powers were such that, as in the case of Sallé, expression made mere physical execution seem unimportant.

This does not mean that Guimard had technical difficulties. It simply means that, in spite of the fact that she was equipped for the *danse noble*, she preferred the *danse demi-caractère,* that she never, in the words of Noverre, "courted difficulties" and that "she put expression and feeling into all her movements." But although she was not primarily an executant, she was, in a sense, creative. She

49

did not compose ballets or invent steps but she brought fresh interpretative powers to bear upon repertory pieces.

Along with other dancers, she was noted for lightness and grace, but she had a special flair for combining innocence with voluptuousness, by no means a small feat. This odd and enticing effect she achieved through the introduction of pauses, of slight hesitations. It was, of course, a form of coquetry, but it delighted an audience who could watch Guimard as a shepherdess (her favorite part) move voluptuously, invitingly by herself but hesitating with delicious innocence before she directed her charms in the direction of a swain. A knowing audience, furthermore, was amused by her enactment of a pastoral lass, for in her private life Guimard was the antithesis of such a one. She was rich, extravagant, and sophisticated, and it delighted her and her followers to partake in this theatrical pretense.

A shrewd coquettishness appeared to govern her personal life and attract to her men and even women of power. She tended to fall in love with members of her own profession, but she was far too practical to let her heart rule her head. She wanted money not only because she was extravagant but also because she was generous, and she accepted it from any quarter. She was pursued by admirers but she selected her friends with great care. Either they were incredibly rich (in which case it didn't matter about their appearances) or young, brilliant, and beautiful. Three of the most prominent men of France —a court official, a prince, and a bishop—were her particular patrons.

A party-giver, with a town house, a country house, two private theaters, expensive tastes in clothes, and concern for the poor, needed funds at all times, so it was small wonder that Guimard found it necessary to demand financial assistance from her patrons.

In the little theater (it seated about two hundred) at her country home on the outskirts of Paris, and in the larger theater (with a capacity of five hundred) in her town house, which had been designed by the king's own architect and decorated by the great artist Fragonard, Guimard delighted in presenting programs for the amusement of her guests. Variety in her guest list appealed to her and to this end the ballerina gave three supper parties each week: the first for the aristocracy, the second for artists, and the third for fashionable roués and their equally fashionable female companions.

Guimard, however, was not selfish. During hard days in Paris, she asked one of her patrons to give her cash instead of gifts, and with the money she went to the poor and gave many families enough to supply their wants for a winter and, sometimes, for an entire year. Guimard was just as considerate of her patrons, and when one encountered financial difficulties, she asked him to cancel her allowance (or pension) and saw to it that other dancers at the Opéra who were also receiving financial assistance from him join her in requesting that he cease all payments to them.

Occasionally, Guimard's expenditures rose to such a level that no one could help her out and then it was up to her to find a way out of her difficulties. In one such instance, she was forced to sell her town house by lottery, but apparently no remorse was experienced, for although she liked riches and luxuries, she could get along modestly if she had to. Certainly, when she married late in life, she chose a man of modest circumstances (Jean Despréaux, a poet, choreographer, and long-time friend) and lived contentedly on their joint pensions, on what he earned from time to time, and, when most of their income was gone, in comparative poverty.

Above and beyond everything—wealth, fame, fun—stood her

love of dancing, and it was said that she never missed a performance, never ignored a rehearsal. Neither did she ignore her appearance. Her expensive clothes and costumes were always in perfect
taste, made of the finest materials but devoid of the embellishments
popular at the time. Her face, not pretty but extremely piquant, was
treated with the greatest care. At twenty, she had had her portrait
painted, and this she used as a model for her make-up every day so
that at fifty she looked (perhaps at a distance) as she had when the
portrait was done. Even smallpox, which scarred her face midway
in her career, did not mar this painted prettiness, for at forty, on
stage, she seemed to be barely fifteen years of age.

She was, however, very slender, and a woman with a sharp
tongue once noted that a certain *pas de trois* which Guimard danced
with two men looked like "two dogs quarreling over a bone." Yet
if she was thin and not especially beautiful, she was fascinating
enough to inspire painters and sculptors and to evoke from one a
statement to the effect that "her dancing was sketchy; she only did
little steps but with such graceful movement that the public preferred her to all other dancers."

She was preferred, one can imagine, not only because she was
cute and graceful and sensual but because she had mastered the art
of make-believe. She was an actress. And she lived during that
era when the ballet of mere steps was giving way to the *ballet
d'action*, ballet in which dramatically meaningful movement was
stressed. It is not surprising that Noverre, founder of the *ballet
d'action*, admired her (as he had the older Sallé) extravagantly and
cast her in several of his history-making ballets (*Apelles et Cam-
paspe, Les Caprices de Galathée, Médée et Jason*). Strangely
enough, suited as she was to Noverre's works, she sided against him

in an intrigue at the Opéra and gave her considerable support (she practically directed all activities at the Opéra) to Gardel and Dauberval (the choreographer whose *La Fille Mal Gardée* is still performed).

Throughout her long career, which included her many years as the star at the Opéra, appearances in the French court, and seasons in London, she remained an interpreter. Leaps, *entrechats*, aerial action of all kinds she evaded, but she could move swiftly across the ground without roughness of any kind and this area was sufficient for one who knew the dramatic value of differences in speed, in accent, in intensity; for one whose neck and head and arms and roguish eyes could dance. Once, she attempted to sing along with a dancing part, but movement in silence appeared to be more eloquent than her singing and she refrained from further efforts along this line.

On August 14, 1789, in her forty-sixth year, Madeleine Guimard left behind her the glitter of Parisian and London stages, the opulence of court life. For a time, she and her husband, Despréaux, lived quietly and comfortably, but the coming of the French Revolution worked its hardships on both. Pensions ceased, jobs for the husband were difficult to get, and life in Paris was not easy. But they survived in their little home in Montmartre, and in 1796 Guimard emerged from retirement to make one last public appearance in a benefit for the old-time stars of the Opéra.

But during their declining years, in spite of only sporadic posts (as governments came and went) for the husband, the couple found happiness. Despréaux, after Guimard's death, wrote sweetly and touchingly of one he had known and admired for many years, one who had ultimately become his wife: "It was in the dance *terre à*

MLLE. GUIMARD

terre that Mlle. Guimard delighted a critical audience for over twenty-five years. She was always different. I am not referring only to the charm of the movements of her feet, which were few in comparison with those of her head and body. Therein lies the perfection of the picture—her expressive features depicted with ease the emotions she felt or was supposed to feel."

But even if Guimard's feet were not her distinguishing feature, they brought her joy in her old age. Friends would ask her to dance, but wisely she knew that face and body were not those of the Guimard of old, so her husband hung a curtain which obscured the upper body and thus the old ballerina and her husband, with only feet and legs showing, danced for their circle of friends. Subterfuge perhaps it was, but the onlookers beheld only youth as the ballerina's shapely foot and leg danced vigorously, easily, and still coquettishly beneath the hemline of that curtain which hid the passage of time.

Later, age crept down toward the twinkling feet, and an old lady who could not stop dancing sat with a tiny drum in her lap and with two fingers moving like legs recreated the ballets and the career which had brought beauty and excitement to the theater of dance. On May 14, 1816, the fingers were stilled forever, the drum slipped from the old lap, and the roguish eyes closed upon an epoch.

MARIE TAGLIONI IN "LA SYLPHIDE"

Five

OF THE AIR AND OF THE EARTH

Marie Taglioni, 1804–1884, born in Stockholm, changed the course of ballet history at the Paris Opéra in the world première (1832) of La Sylphide *with movement sur les pointes and the use of romantic themes based upon European legends and tales rather than upon classical Greek mythology. Introducer and symbol of this new age, Taglioni brought the illusion of flight and an air of spirituality to ballet. Retired in 1847.*

57

"Try, Marie, try! That's it. Higher, reach higher into the air." The small but strong feet pushed away from the ground, rose to the ball of the foot, pressed upward until the girl was standing on her toes, not the flat of the toes but the tips, standing *sur les pointes*. Perhaps this scene never actually occurred. Perhaps another dancer was the first to discover the miracle of *la pointe*. But it was Marie Taglioni who lifted the ballet out of the stagnation of its tired pseudo-Greek classicism and into those fresh currents of air which breathed of romance, mystery, and spirituality.

"To your feet and to your wings," wrote Victor Hugo. And Taglioni had wings, not only those sewed to her costume in her immortal *La Sylphide* but also wings in her feet which bore her swiftly into the air and delayed her descent to earth. Even her *arabesque* gave the impression of flight. As she moved on her toes in soft, unblocked (but darned) toe slippers, she ceased to walk and, thereby, raised the ballerina to a mystical plane where, in lovely unreality, she could float and glide above the tramping, earthbound mortal.

Keats, penning "Thou still unravished bride of quietness," might well have been describing Taglioni, the virginal dancer, a fragile figure whose angel wings would make brief contact with harsh humanity. But this was her theme and the theme of her age: reality in conflict with unreality; dreams, ideals fighting fact. Through ballet, she joined the poets and playwrights and painters and novelists in celebrating the fresh hopes of man, and in her ballets the vulnerability of soaring, exposed beauty, like a bird on the wing, was tragically revealed.

This unearthly dance beauty which was Taglioni's, this gentle power which had Europe at her feet, this hypnotic emanation which compelled a fanatical group of her followers to boil her toe slippers and eat them as a toast to her genius, were the property of a frail, round-shouldered girl who had once been refused by a teacher who did not know "what to do with that little hunchback." But dancing was in the blood of one who belonged to a family of dancers and who could not be stopped by scrawniness or by lack of beauty.

Her grandfather had been a dancer, and her aunts and uncles and father, too, were dancers. The heritage of Italian dance, volatile and full of virtuosity, was hers, but so also were the influences— cool, emotionally disciplined, idealistic—of her mother's native Sweden. It was her father, Philippe Taglioni, however, who trained her from the start and guided her entire career. It was he who lifted the thin and sagging shoulders, devised positions to conceal the unusual length of her arms, invented sequences of leaping, flying movements to display that aerial range which was Marie's special province.

Father Taglioni had come to Stockholm as ballet master for the Royal Opera. To his surprise, he discovered that his new charges were fifty years behind the times, that they were still wearers of hoop skirts, lofty wigs, and heeled shoes. Through his great gifts as a teacher and choreographer, he helped to modernize this Scandinavian ballet, but while he was serving here and in the other capitals of Europe, much of his interests and energies went out to the daughter who was to be by his side for almost all the remaining years of his life.

When Marie was just about eighteen, her father arranged for her debut at Vienna in a work propitiously titled *The Reception of a Young Nymph at the Court of Terpsichore*. For this occasion, he designed the choreography for his daughter, but so nervous was she that she forgot her steps and was forced to improvise on stage. Everything turned out for the best, however, for the young dancer had such a successful debut that some of the more experienced stars of Viennese ballet were, temporarily at least, forgotten.

Following her professional bow in 1822, Taglioni continued her travels with her father, appearing in his companies, performing to enthusiastic response in Stuttgart, and dancing with her younger brother (born in 1808), who, years later, with his wife as partner, was to carry the Taglioni name across the seas to America. Finally, in 1827, the father arranged for his daughter and son to make their Paris debuts at the temple of dance itself, the Opéra. Appearing in a special duet inserted into *Le Sicilien*, the two made successful if not particularly spectacular impressions upon the French public.

Marie, as a regular member of the Paris Opéra, continued to dance in the company's regular repertory. The old-fashioned ballets, however, did little to reveal her special talent. She was thoroughly trained, of course, in the techniques and the traditions of the classical ballet, but she was not particularly good at mime and her sweet spirituality had no opportunity to shimmer in those cold *divertissements* strung along a mythological theme. Even if she had not yet found her forte, she was highly admired. The great composer Rossini composed a Tyrolienne for her in his opera *William Tell*, and another composer, Auber, created an opera-ballet, *Le Dieu et la Bayadère*, with her in mind.

The London press and public were also stirred by her dancing and, on the occasion of her English debut, cheered her lustily and commented, "We have never seen her equal." She had a taste of the kind of dancing she sought in the opera *Robert le Diable*, where she led a fantastic ballet of nuns, but the moment the dance world was unknowingly awaiting did not come until March 12, 1832, when *La Sylphide* was given its world première at the Paris Opéra. On that date, an era ended and a new dance epoch commenced. Jupiter, Juno, Diana, and their Olympian colleagues died and gave way to sylphs, pixies, peris, sprites, and creatures of dreams.

Choreographed by Philippe Taglioni, *La Sylphide* told the story of a Scottish youth awakened by the kiss of a Sylph who fades away as dream fades into consciousness. Later, at a peasant party celebrating his betrothal to a village maid, he sees the Sylph (although she is invisible to the others) floating about and pursues her to the forest. There she performs her elusive dance with him in a clearing where witches and then a bevy of sylphs had previously danced their measures. Snatching an enchanted scarf given to him by a disguised witch, he throws it about the fragile Sylph and she expires just as a wedding group, headed by his former sweetheart and her new mate, passes by. He, too, dies and is borne away by a company of sylphs.

By our standards of today, this may appear to be a quaint and not especially stirring fairy tale. But it threw Paris into a delighted uproar. At last something novel had come to destroy the boredom generated by the frigid, acrobatic, thematically sterile ballets, with their forgotten gods and goddesses of antiquity, of the regular repertory. Here was a new way of dance, new dance materials, new costumes and settings, a new way of using *pointes*, new emotional colorings, newness everywhere.

The costume itself—a white and soft bell-like skirt, tight bodice, and off-shoulder cut of the dress—became the classical ballet apparel. The temples of classical Greece disappeared and gave way to ruined castles, misty glades, moonlit waters, regions of fantasy.

Leg-beats were no longer examples of technical display but the flutterings of an air-borne creature; the *arabesque* was no more a feat of balance but a vision of poised waiting; and the rising on the toes became the symbol of transport to another world.

Just as everything had once become *à la Camargo* in the fashion life of Paris, so now modes and products were classified *à la Sylphide*. England followed Paris in its acclaim of *La Sylphide*, and such was Taglioni's fame that on an incognito visit to Scotland, she was recognized by townsfolk as the one who had used their country as the locale for her epoch-making ballet and they asked her to dance for them. She complied, not with *La Sylphide* but with the dance of a milkmaid.

The Sylphide influence spread. It was to be found in her father's *La Laitière Suisse* and *La Fille du Danube* (in which she danced a water nymph) ; in *La Péri, Ondine*, and a ballet which has continued triumphantly down the years, *Giselle*; in *Swan Lake, Les Sylphides*, and other ballets present in current repertories. Wherever Taglioni went with *La Sylphide* and further ballets designed for her by her father, she was treated as a veritable "Queen of the Dance." Austrian noblemen unhitched the horses from her carriage and pulled her in triumph through the streets of Vienna. Crowds, clawing, fighting, and trampling one another, tried to catch the flowers she tossed from her balcony. France, Germany, Austria, Russia, Italy, England were at her feet.

In her private life, she appeared to be modest, virtuous, and highly intelligent (she spoke many languages fluently), but much of it was sad. Marriage to the Count de Voisins terminated unhappily after two children and three years. Her life ended in a state of abject poverty and she saw the career of her beloved pupil,

Emma Livry, for whom she choreographed her only ballet, *Le Papillon*, cut short almost at its glorious start by death caused when her costume caught fire in rehearsal.

But whatever her private life, with its virtuousness and sadness and joys, was like, her professional behavior turned heads gray. She was greedy for money, jealous of potential rivals, demanding, and difficult. It was this very attitude which gave her greatest and only rival the opportunity she needed, for if Taglioni had not been so imperious and difficult, the director of the Paris Opéra might never have engaged Fanny Elssler to serve as a sort of threat to the now unpredictable Marie. But Fanny was hired and her success was so enormous that, although she did not succeed in unseating Taglioni from her throne, she did cause Paris to divide itself into taglionistes and elssleristes.

Taglioni could surely have held her own indefinitely in any such competition, but she was not one to gamble. Elssler had made her Opéra debut in 1834 and two years later, with the introduction of her sensational, fiery Cachucha, she became a genuine danger, for it was then that the elssleristes were formed. The following year, 1837, Taglioni bowed out of the picture in Paris after ten years with the Opéra. She was taking no chances and, besides, there were other places ready for conquest. Elssler, too, had been uneasy —nay, frightened—about appearing in the same company with Taglioni and had studied furiously before her first Parisian performance.

Once separated, the two were surer of themselves, even defiant, for Elssler later attempted to dance *La Sylphide* in Paris (and a failure it was) and Taglioni, safely away in Russia, essayed something of Elssler's earthy, fiery province with *La Gitana*. But Russia

63

was by no means subjected to a Taglioni determined to imitate Elssler. She gave them of her light and ethereal best in old ballets and new (such as *L'Ombre*, created for her by her father) and like France and England, Russia made her the toast of a nation.

For three years she remained. Fashions and gadgets were named for her; the Czar left the imperial box the better to see her from the orchestra floor; the fine dancers of the Russian ballet learned so much from her that, when she left, a native Russian was prepared to dance ballerina roles in the new style. It was here that, on her departure, a group of devoted fans cooked and ate her dancing shoes, made more palatable, one supposes, by the addition of a special sauce.

Triumphs in Italy in 1841 followed, and in 1845 she participated in one of the most celebrated ballet performances of all time, a command performance in London for Queen Victoria. She had always been a favorite of the Queen, who as a young girl had shown her admiration of the ballerina by having a Taglioni doll as a plaything, and on this occasion Taglioni consented to join forces with Grisi, Grahn, and Cerito, three of the top ballerinas of the day, in a *Pas de Quatre* especially choreographed for the four great ballerinas, rich in temperament as well as talent.

Two years later, in 1847, twenty-five years after her debut in Vienna, Marie Taglioni, at the age of forty-three, made her farewell in London. That same year in that same city a Maria Taglioni, niece of the great Marie, launched a successful career which was to continue a dancing dynasty for yet another generation. But Marie herself, though no longer a performer, remained close to the art throughout the long and hard thirty-seven years of life left to her.

At first she rested, settling with her father at Lake Como, but she taught and she advised and she guided younger dancers because she wanted to do so. Later, she was forced to teach when her considerable savings were wiped out during the Franco-Prussian War. Poor and aging, she journeyed to London to teach grace and deportment to the young of the aristocracy. She lost her money, she lost her loved Livry, her father died, her son was taken as a prisoner of war, and bitterness settled upon the heart of one whose dancing had been the symbol of aspiration, of dreams, of flight. Forgotten, she died in Marseilles. The year was 1884 and Marius Petipa (creator of *Swan Lake*) was already a master choreographer and a new star, light and ethereal as Taglioni, Anna Pavlova, had already been born.

But Taglioni had made possible a Petipa and a Pavlova. She had revolutionized ballet in her time and so thoroughly had she done it that the romantic pieces of her period became the classics of the next, the models for classical dances for a century to come. The ballerina, long in the ascent theatrically, became with Taglioni supreme. Men were no longer needed except as adjuncts to the choreography, as dramatic necessities. Woman, frail and pure and desirable, was deified in the ballerina.

The new style reinforced a tradition that each ballerina not only had to beat her rivals but had to surpass herself of yesterday with new steps and new tricks, new virtuosities. Woman, idealized, could not rest on an ideal. She had to have ideas. Taglioni had them, soaring ideas which bore her and her adoring followers on winged feet through groves and glades, beneath the blue of the waters, into moon-caressed skies, across carpets of unbruised flowers, into magical worlds, into aspiring hearts.

Fanny Elssler, 1810–1884, Viennese-born ballerina, a fiery artist, described as the "pagan dancer." She was the exact opposite of the spiritual Taglioni and Taglioni's only rival. The earthiness of folk dancing was stressed in her ballets and she achieved one of her greatest successes with the lively Cachucha in Le Diable Boiteux, presented at the Paris Opéra in 1836. Retired in 1851.

FANNY ELSSLER
IN "THE GYPSY"

Fanny Elssler, Taglioni's rival, was of the earth. Not for her the nebulousness of clouds, the fragile wings of the sylph. Her rounded arms, her silken legs, her fine bosom were of this world. She, too, was the ideal woman, but earthly, desirable, and, perhaps, obtainable. The spiritual Taglioni had been called, because of her ethereal quality, the "Christian dancer," so it followed that Elssler, nature's child, was named the "pagan dancer."

This "pagan" creature, only a few years younger than Taglioni, was born in Vienna (1810) but not into a dancing family. Her father was a musician, associated in a modest way with the composer Haydn, and her mother was an expert seamstress, an embroiderer. But dancing, if not in Fanny's blood, was in her soul, and by the time she was seven she had made a sufficiently impressive debut to warrant further study and the planning of a career. Ironically enough, she took part in the formal debut of one who was to become her greatest and only rival, for little Fanny was in the *corps de ballet* the night that Taglioni was presented to Vienna and the dance world in *The Reception of a Young Nymph at the Court of Terpsichore*.

While still in her teens, she joined a traveling Italian troupe and went to Italy. Here, far away from the strict and cool classicism of Viennese ballet, she found opportunity (and encouragement) to add greater fervor and fire to her dancing, to develop a personal style. Three years later, upon her return to northern climes, she was ready to rouse her audiences. Together with her sister, Thérèse, she danced in Berlin with notable success, and when she reached Vienna again, Philippe Taglioni (the great Marie's father) produced *La Laitière Suisse* especially for this rising star. Now commenced the comparisons with Taglioni, but although Elssler was praised for her superior pantomime, the senior artist was still untouchable.

Like many a ballerina before her, Elssler had a patron, a gentleman interested in fostering the advancement of a gifted girl. The old nobleman saw to her education and treated her handsomely and kindly until his death. With his passing and the death of her mother, the bereaved Fanny found comfort in the love of a fellow dancer. They had a daughter, but neither romance nor motherhood could long delay her progress and soon she was off to London, where, in 1833, she appeared at Covent Garden, often dancing during her season there on the same bills with Taglioni. Again comparisons were made, but the elder remained the favorite while her junior, with admittedly greater "resources" as a beauty and as an actress, won the admiration of press and public.

By 1834, it was clear that, in Elssler, Taglioni had a genuine rival, and Veron, director of the Paris Opéra, who was worried that Taglioni would become increasingly outrageous in her demands as her star rose higher and higher, sought to engage Elssler for the Opéra. With this end in view, he gave an elaborate banquet for the Elssler sisters (Fanny and Thérèse) and culminated the feast with offerings of jewels from which they could make selections. They were not to be bribed, however, and so they selected modest mementoes of the occasion. But they did, finally, agree to sign contracts with Veron. A nervous Fanny, nevertheless, would not agree to perform until she had had three months of intensive study with the celebrated male dancer, Auguste Vestris, who, as a onetime temperamental and highly personal virtuoso, must certainly have delighted in the lively, flamboyant dancing of his illustrious pupil.

Debut time came and Elssler appeared in *La Tempête*, a dull and dreary dance version of the Shakespearean play. Success was instantaneous and the elssleristes commenced to form, but just as Taglioni had been forced to wait for the perfect vehicle, so Elssler bided her time for two seasons. Then, in 1836, came the production of *Le Diable Boiteux*, a ballet with a Spanish setting, and in it was the Cachucha.

This was history, for although national dances had been introduced into ballets before, they had been classicized and sterilized so thoroughly that they would have been wholly unrecognizable to the inhabitants of their countries of origin. Not so with Elssler. She let her castanets rap out the rhythms of Spain, her feet made magical contacts with the earth, and her full, lush body swayed and dipped and bent and preened. Now the elssleristes were ready to do battle for their idol, for another new and exciting way of dance, a new type of ballet, had been born.

Elssler found her formula. Almost all of Taglioni's later successes were modeled after *La Sylphide*, and with Elssler, the pattern was implicit in *Le Diable Boiteux*. *The Gypsy*, *La Tarentule*, and the many ballets and *divertissements* which followed found the "divine Fanny" as a Spaniard, a Pole, a Russian, a Hungarian as she brought to the theater not dreams or spiritual aspirations but the bright colors of nationalties, the earthy energy of the folk, the real zest of the really living. And if Taglioni became the model of the classic ballerina, Elssler instituted the balletic art of the character dancer.

The rivalry in the two camps was sharp. The taglionistes prevailed upon Vestris to come out of retirement and dance a simple *pas* with Taglioni. At the close, the former God of the Dance, as he had been called in his dancing youth, was to crown Taglioni Goddess of the Dance, but before the crowning took place, the orchestra, given the wrong cue, struck up the band with the wrong music and the deification failed to occur. Who gave the cue? Elssler? An elssleriste? Or perhaps even Vestris himself, teacher of Elssler, could not be certain which was the true goddess.

Upon Taglioni's departure from the Opéra, the triumphant Fanny attempted not only *La Sylphide* but also Taglioni's *La Fille du Danube* and got thoroughly hissed for her efforts. Thereafter, she wisely refrained from further encroaching tactics and returned to her own ballets, among them *La Volière*, choreographed by her sister, in which Thérèse appeared as a boy (the final insult to the male dancer).

With a brief leave of absence granted, Elssler said good-bye to the Paris Opéra in the rousing new *La Smolenska*, traveled to London for another hearty adieu, and set sail for America and one of the most exciting passages in her life or in the life of any artist.

Americans had been warned through their press that Elssler was "Somebody" and that the European opinion of America's cultural level would hinge to a great extent upon the proper response to the continental favorite. America disappointed neither Europe nor Elssler, and she, although she was frightened of the venture, did not disappoint her new public. She opened in New York at the Park Theater in *La Cracovienne* and *La Tarentule*. But before she could dance, the whole house rose and applauded. During the program, loud shouts of delight greeted her feats of skill, and as the curtain fell, a "roar" of approval, showers of flowers, and wreaths hailed a new American favorite.

Her performances at the Park saved the theater manager from bankruptcy. Her mere presence, as an audience member, in a theater assured a sold-out house. President Van Buren's son was her escort and society opened its careful doors to her. Fanny had conquered

New York but she was also to capture all of America. She ignored the time specification of her leave of absence from the Paris Opéra and remained in the New World for two years. Baltimore, not to be outdone by the tribute the Viennese paid to Taglioni, witnessed a scene in which romantic young gentlemen pulled the Elssler carriage through the streets. In Washington, so many federal legislators planned to see her perform that Congress was adjourned. Later, the ballerina was received at the White House by the President and his cabinet, and at a banquet in her honor, wine was drunk from her dancing slipper. In Philadelphia, New Orleans, Boston, the treatment reserved for royalty was repeated again and again. The thrifty, businesslike star accepted with delight these attentions and all the money she could get—thousands of dollars a week—but she was shrewd, too, and in gratitude gave a tidy sum toward the construction of a monument on Bunker Hill.

After two years of performing in America and Cuba, she returned, perhaps reluctantly, to Europe. Behind her she left an adoring public, a nation flooded with lithographs of her, sheet music bearing her picture, and a state of dance which, strangely enough, was left uninfluenced by her powerful presence and innovations.

The Paris Opéra was closed to her because of her naughtiness in staying away so long, but the rest of Europe was hers. In Russia, where she remained for several seasons, she was acclaimed as thoroughly as Taglioni had been. She made her debut (1848) in *Giselle* at St. Petersburg, later adding yet other new ballets to her regular repertory. In Moscow she earned more laurels, and by the time she was ready to leave Russia she had left her mark upon the ballet, particularly in the person of the young choreographer, Marius Petipa. And here one might pause to reflect upon the unbroken and highly personal chronology of ballet performing and training. Sallé, who had studied with Prévost, danced once with the young Gaetan Vestris, whose son Auguste (as an old man) had been Elssler's instructor. Now, in Russia, Elssler was bringing her inherited knowledge as well as her personal innovations to Petipa, the master of many ballerinas, the choreographer whose contemporary heir is Balanchine, chief choreographer of the New York City Ballet.

As she had promised, Fanny Elssler retired while she was still at the peak of her powers, still beautiful, still wanted. At forty-one, in her native Vienna, she made her farewell (1851) in a ballet version of *Faust*. With plenty of money saved, she lived quietly in Vienna or nearby, loved by her friends, remembered and respected by the company of artistic people with whom she associated. Contentedly, she died in 1884, the same year that her worthy rival, Taglioni, passed from bitter loneliness to the peace of that heaven toward which she was always soaring.

While Taglioni had bequeathed the heritage of flight to the dancer, Elssler left a bequest of flashing energy. Taglioni was to be reborn in a Pavlova and a Markova. Elssler would find her immortality in the provocative moments of a Danilova or a Slavenska. But actually, neither won the crown of crowns in the generations to follow any more than she did in life. For while they were yet alive, their highly individual discoveries were being fused so that a ballerina, such as Carlotta Grisi, would have to shine in both areas within the framework of a single ballet, *Giselle*. And as time passed by, the classical dance adopted the rhythms and the steps of the folk dance while retaining the purity of the little-changing *danse d'école* and the elusive, flying loveliness of the woman-ideal, personified in Taglioni.

CARLOTTA GRISI IN
"LA PÉRI"

A WILI, A NAIAD, A DRYAD

Carlotta Grisi, 1819–1899, Italian-born and Italian-trained bal-
lerina. In 1841, at the Paris Opéra, she created her most famous
role, the heroine of Giselle, a ballet which demanded of the bal-
lerina the earthiness of Elssler and the spirituality of Taglioni. Re-
tired to Switzerland in 1854.

When Taglioni ushered in the Romantic age of ballet with *La Sylphide*, she let loose a rash of fairy-like creatures which (or who) were to invade the realm of dance for years to come. Three great ballerinas of this era, younger contemporaries of Taglioni and Elssler, could not, even if they would, escape the spell of sprites and pixies. Carlotta Grisi found her greatest role and her claim to immortality in *Giselle*, in which she danced the part of a Wili (Act II), the restless ghost of a maiden who had died before her wedding day. In *Ondine*, Fanny Cerito had her very favorite part, that of a nereid or sea nymph, and Lucile Grahn rounded out the picture with her dryad, the woodland sprite of *Eoline*.

The three earned continental and English acclaim in these and other ballets, some of them concerned with fairy beings and others with flesh-and-blood characters. But perhaps their greatest moment came when they were united with Taglioni in the Victorian *Pas de Quatre*. This unprecedented event, the uniting in a single *divertisse-ment* of four of the greatest stars of the day, almost failed to ma-terialize, Queen Victoria's command to the contrary. Precedence was the problem, for although Taglioni was given, without any argument by the others, the place of honor with the last solo before the finale, Grisi, Cerito, and Grahn battled about who should be next in importance. No one wanted to be first with her solo. Rehearsals were deadlocked; Perrot, the choreographer, was helpless; then the manager entered the fray and announced that age would determine the precedence. Three ladies argued no further.

The performance itself delighted everyone and, aside from some minor displays of favoritism among small groups of ardent partisans, the event went off smoothly and the ballerinas behaved nicely to each other. Cerito even went so far as to offer a tossed wreath as a crown to Taglioni. So if there was venom present, it was concealed, but one may be certain that each danced as she never did before. Critics were almost wholly impartial, lauding the beloved Taglioni and remarking upon the beauty of her gentle propulsion through space; praising Grahn, who belonged to the Taglioni style of dance; delighting in the fleet and piquant actions of Grisi; and exclaiming over Cerito's revolving leaps.

Since its revival (one version by Anton Dolin and one by Keith Lester) nearly a century later, the *Pas de Quatre* has been danced by minor artists, soloists, and ballerinas. Among those who have danced it as an all-star affair in our own time are Markova, Baronova, Kaye, and Annabelle Lyon and Markova, Danilova, Slavenska, and Nathalie Krassovska. In the revivals, the sweet graciousness is present but hints of jealous hauteur are allowed to creep into the characterizations by way of adding spice to a period piece. And one may suppose that each contemporary ballerina, while she is dancing, imagines that she really is (or is as good as) Taglioni, Grisi, Grahn, or Cerito.

Of the three—Grisi, Grahn, Cerito—Grisi's name has meant the most to succeeding generations of dancers mainly because she was the first to dance a ballet which is still in the repertories of the major ballet companies, still a box-office draw, still the *"Hamlet* of the dance," still a work to test the mettle of the ballerina. It was June 28, 1841, when the curtain of the Paris Opéra first rose on *Giselle*. Grisi was already a member of the Opéra and, with Taglioni and Elssler in other parts of the earth, she was the reigning star.

The poet Gautier had written the story of *Giselle*, Adolphe Adam had composed the delectable score, and Coralli was credited with the choreography. Among the announced credits one name was missing, that of Jules Perrot; yet written comments of the day made it quite clear that Perrot, Grisi's husband, had arranged all of her scenes and dances for her, leaving the rest of the ballet to Coralli. But it was Grisi who transformed an obviously great ballet into a personal triumph.

The critics spoke of her perfection; of her lightness, freedom, and "delicate abandon"; of her enormous pantomimic skill, which did not rely upon one conventional gesture; of her incredible *tours de force*, which were accomplished effortlessly; of her originality. They found her to be as light as Taglioni and as lively as Elssler, an individual artist whose expressional medium lay between the two dance extremes exploited by the senior ballerinas. Furthermore, it was reported, perhaps a trifle inaccurately, that Grisi was either in air or on toe throughout the ballet. *"Giselle,"* according to one, was *"La Sylphide* without a moment's rest."

Giselle had, truly, sought to combine the discoveries of Taglioni and Elssler. The first act had its joyous peasant dances, and Giselle herself, as a peasant maid, took part pantomimically and in dance in the lively, pastoral proceedings. Here, too, in the culminating mad scene, the ballerina had to bring to the fore her acting skills as she broke furiously away from her noble and somewhat deceitful lover to dance and act out her poignant death by suicide. With Act II, she had become a wraith, one of an army of maidens who had died before their nuptials and were destined to haunt the midnight hours. As a Wili, the ballerina had to portray the unreal, the elusive, the fairy creature and, in this capacity, entice the mourning, repentant lover into a frenzied dance of death. Yet as a heroine she had to indicate that earthly love had not been entirely chilled by death and that if she could have him no longer she would at least seek to save him from death at the hands of the other Wilis.

This monumental task of characterization and dancing Grisi accomplished in triumph. But she had not arrived at the most difficult of ballet assignments unprepared. As the precocious child of a distinguished musical family, she had commenced ballet study in her native Italy when she was only seven and had worn herself out in no time at all by responding enthusiastically to the endless requests that she perform. For a while, she rested her fragile body and studied singing, but the urgent voice of dance called and soon she was touring Italy as a dancer.

In 1834, when she was only fifteen, she joined Cerito as a *prima ballerina* with the San Carlo Opera in Naples and was illustrious enough, at that tender age, to have a ballet especially mounted for her. The following year she met Perrot (later to become her husband) and became both his partner and his pupil. Together they traveled to London to make, in 1836, a successful English debut in *Le Rossignol*. The English found her attractive, agile, and "a mixture of the impassioned and the graceful." Even more successful was *Tarentella* and an unusual presentation found her singing (in a fair but not remarkable voice) as well as dancing.

There followed a brief appearance in Paris (not at the Opéra, for she had not yet been invited there) and tours to Vienna, Milan, and Munich during which Grisi appeared in Perrot's ballets and other works, including *La Sylphide*. After a spell of hard, intensive training, Carlotta Grisi made her debut at the Paris Opéra (1840) as soloist in the opera *La Favorite*. A new princess of dance was discovered, and with the production of *Giselle* the following year, the princess became the queen.

Everyone fell in love with her, among them the poet Gautier and the young and handsome Lucien Petipa (brother of Marius), her partner in *Giselle*. One success followed another. First, there was *La Jolie Fille de Gand;* next *La Péri,* almost as popular as *Giselle* and a ballet in which Grisi jumped from a cloud into the waiting (and sturdy) arms of Petipa (as an old lady of sixty, she vowed she could still accomplish this acrobatic feat); then *Le Diable à Quatre;* and finally *Paquita,* a ballet which was to get transplanted to Russia and ultimately be restaged (in a shortened version) in American by Danilova.

In 1849 she said farewell to the Paris Opéra and shortly thereafter set out, as did Taglioni and Elssler, to conquer Russia. She chose *Giselle* for her debut and so frequently did she perform it during the course of her stay that Marius Petipa was able to study it thoroughly and a half-century later teach it, as its originator had done it, to a young artist named Anna Pavlova.

At thirty-five, Grisi retired to Switzerland with her daughter and settled down to a quiet life with her embroidery, and in 1899, no longer boasting that she could accomplish the leap from *La Péri,* she died.

79

FANNY CERITO IN "ONDINE"

Fanny Cerito, 1821–1899?, a native of Naples, made her debut in that city in 1834. One of her greatest popular successes was her dancing of the Daughter of Fire in Alma in 1842 (London), but history has identified her with Ondine, a ballet in which she devised some of the choreography. Retired in 1855.

A great shell slowly rises from the sea. Framed by its delicate pinkness is Ondine, daughter of the Queen of the Waters. Thus Fanny Cerito, contemporary of Grisi, appeared to an audience in her favorite ballet, *Ondine*. In quest of the love of a fisherman, the sea nymph flew through open windows, opened her arms invitingly as she sank gently into the waves, pretended to be a mortal, and almost died. In the moonlight, she discovered her shadow for the first time and, believing it to be her rival, pursued it in a fleet and eerie dance. This was romance and fantasy, and the public loved it. The public also loved Fanny, "La Divinita," as she was called by her adoring father. By some standards, she was considered short and plump; by others, tiny and rounded; but almost everyone agreed that she was a "trinity of grace, strength, suppleness."

An Italian girl, radiating happiness and energy, Fanny had made her debut in the ballet *L'Oroscopo* (1834) in her home city of Naples and four years later was sharing ballerina honors with Grisi in Milan. By 1840, she was in London, that second capital of ballet, where, two years later, she enjoyed her greatest success in *Alma* as the Daughter of Fire. But the next season's *Ondine*, critical comments to the contrary, was even more important to her, for she had choreographed portions of it herself. In the succeeding years, *La Vivandière, Rosida, La Fille du Marbe,* and *Gemma* (wholly choreographed by the ballerina) added further glory to a star hailed in England, France, and even distant Russia, in Spain, Austria, and the other nations she graced with her spirited presence.

No career in those days would have been complete without an engagement at the Paris Opéra, without the approval of the French public and press. Fanny achieved both goals, for the Paris of 1847 adored her in *La Fille du Marbe*, choreographed by her husband and (ofttimes) partner, Arthur Saint-Léon. Everything, from her handsome bust through her "unusual attitudes" to her bounding speed, was admired. In 1855, with her final Paris appearance behind her, she set forth for Russia and the abrupt end of a shining career.

By the time she reached St. Petersburg, times had changed and public reactions were different. Taglioni, Elssler, and Grisi had already come, been seen, and conquered, and the novelty of a visit by a star of the Paris Opéra had worn a trifle thin. Furthermore, the Russians were commencing to produce their own dance artists, and national pride, understandably enough, tempered their enthusiasm for dance dignitaries from abroad. Cerito, nevertheless, was warmly if not ecstatically received, and if an accident had not occurred, she might well have won Russian hearts as she had the hearts of others.

In rehearsal, a piece of scenery caught fire and fell upon her. The ballerina was, miraculously, uninjured, but the fright gripped her heart with such violence that the weakened organ would no longer permit a still vital body to leap and revolve about the stage. So, like Ondine sinking gently out of view, Fanny Cerito left the theater forever. Her tempestuousness, occasional jealousies, and vibrant muscles were quieted as Fanny took up residence in Paris as a shopkeeper. There she lived with her dreams of past conquests, with modesty, and, perhaps, with quiet happiness until she rejoined, presumably in the same year (1899), her onetime colleague, Carlotta Grisi, this time in the finality of death.

Lucile Grahn, 1821–1907, made her first debut with the Royal Opera in her native Copenhagen (1835) and a triumphant debut at the Paris Opéra in Le Carnaval de Venise *(1838). Although her most famous role was that of the dryad in* Eoline, *she was noted for her versatility. Together with Taglioni, Grisi, and Cerito, she appeared in the historical "Pas de Quatre," given in London (1845) by command of Queen Victoria. Retired in 1848.*

In the delicately tinted lithograph, she flies forever in the clouds, a soft breeze stirring her skirt, flowers dropping from her fingers. This is Eoline, the dryad. This is Lucile Grahn, the fourth ballerina of the unforgettable *Pas de Quatre*. In life, she had been as lovely, as perfect; for those who saw *Eoline* more than a hundred years ago, Grahn was almost the equal of Taglioni. She was light, she was effortless, she was precise, she possessed "consummate skill." As the delicate dryad of *Eoline* or as the musket-bearing bandit queen of *Catarina*, Grahn brought to her dancing the most prodigious classical technique of an era.

To Lucile Grahn, nothing was impossible and little frightened her. She danced a wood nymph or a female musketeer with equal ease; she could act as well as release herself from the force of gravity with springs which bore her high into the air; she gambled her reputation when, as a dancer schooled in the aerial style of Taglioni, she dared to appear with her in the *Pas de Quatre*, and she surely took her life in her hands when she danced the nearly sacred *La Sylphide* at the Paris Opéra itself. In all, she was completely successful, meeting her rivals fearlessly and easily, and she was not defeated until a new star, not associated with the ballet, put her out of business.

Grahn was a Dane, born in Copenhagen in 1821. When she was nine, she commenced her ballet studies in this Scandinavian dance center and made her debut at the Royal Opera when she was fourteen. It is probable that her initial appearance was in *La Muette de Portici*, a ballet which would one day serve Pavlova as the plot for her only feature film. But Copenhagen was not Paris, and after Grahn had appeared in her homeland in traditional and new ballets (including two on Nordic themes), she headed for the Paris Opéra, where she made a triumphant debut in 1838 in *Le Carnaval de Venise*. The second year witnessed her conquest of *La Sylphide*. In the third year, an injury occured which caused her to leave the stage temporarily and the Paris Opéra forever.

But Russia (where she danced *Giselle*) and, especially, England were waiting to see the tall, slender blonde with the "buoyant energy." England was her center, as it became later for another great Danish dancer, Adeline Genée, and it was England that cheered her *Eoline*, *Catarina*, and *Le Jugement de Paris*, in which she appeared with Taglioni and Cerito. Grahn could face competition in her own field but not even she could rival Jenny Lind, the nightingale, the sensation of London. The *prima donna* had made the public forget the *prima ballerina*, so in 1848 Lucile Grahn gave up the unequal struggle and retired to live quietly into the next century, with sixty more years of life to fill out.

An age of great dancing was over, the *Pas de Quatre* was for-

LUCILE GRAHN IN "CATARINA"

gotten, nymphs and dryads and spirit-maidens were sinking into a routine, and Western Europe would not see the like of a Grisi, Grahn, and Cerito, of a Taglioni and an Elssler until Russia sent forth its goddesses of the dance to enchant the world a half-century later. Only the lithographs remained to evoke, briefly and prettily, the magical beauties of the Romantic age.

That the era ushered in by Marie Taglioni had been a great one, no one could deny. She, or an unknown contemporary, had introduced dancing on the tips of the toes, thereby opening up a whole new area of dance action. With the creation of such Romantic ballets as *La Sylphide* and *Giselle*, a two-hundred-year period during which themes based on Greek mythology had been worked, reworked, and thoroughly exhausted came to an end and a dance age characterized by new themes and new ideals as well as by a new technique came into being.

And this age of Taglioni, Elssler, Cerito, Grisi, and Grahn was not simply of interest to a small, select group of ballet lovers. These ballerinas were the genuine stars of their day, queens of the great opera houses of Europe, popular favorites with audiences in every land in which they appeared. As the nineteenth-century equivalents of movie stars and pin-up girls, their days were, of course, numbered, but as serious artists, their contributions to the art of ballet were enduring.

PHILADELPHIAN BALLERINAS

Augusta Maywood, 1825–?, Philadelphia-born dancer, was the first American to be admitted to the Académie Royale de la Danse in Paris and the first American ballerina to gain international fame.

Bluenoses and blue laws to the contrary, America has always had time for theater and for dance. For a very long time it was shy about producing its own stars and Europe did nothing at all to dispel this inferiority complex among the citizens of the New World. Were they not a lot of uncultured farmers and woodsmen, rough pioneers, barbarians? Yet Europe did not consider them barbaric enough to frighten away visitors in search of performing opportunities, in quest of money.

In colonial times, dancers arrived to perform and to teach (we even had dancers of our own), and by the time the Revolutionary War was over, a century of artistic invasion—by French, English, Austrian, Italian, Polish, and Russian dancers—had begun. Hornpipes and acrobatics, pastoral scenes and patriotic ballets flooded the stages until Europe was ready to export the ideas, some of the ballets, and a few of the ballerinas of the new and exciting Romantic age. The junior Taglionis, Elsslers, and others landed on these shores but American dancers were not to be outdone. They were willing to dance in the locally recruited *corps* of the visiting dignitaries but a few wished to be stars themselves and one audacious lass determined to turn the tables and conquer Europe. She did.

AUGUSTA MAYWOOD

Augusta Maywood, destined to become the first American to be admitted to the Académie Royale de la Danse in Paris and the first (and, for more than one hundred years, the only) internationally renowned American ballerina, was born in 1825 into a family of actors. This precocious child, trained in Philadelphia by a French ballet master who had settled there, made her triumphant debut in that city when she was only eleven and, two years later, went on to New York to win the adoration of everyone. She did recitations, she acted, she mimed, but above all she danced with a muscular strength and a personal verve unexpected in a child. At eleven, Philadelphians had seen her in *Le Dieu et la Bayadère* (or *The Maid of Cashmere*), and at fifteen, Parisians were watching her as a *première danseuse* on the sacred stage of the Paris Opéra.

The Paris of 1839 adored the little Augusta as much as Philadelphia and New York had. She was new, she was different, and she was very good, good enough to compare with Taglioni, Elssler, and Grahn, different enough in style to compare with the male dancers of the day. For little Augusta was as strong and as flexible as a young animal, as lively as a circus performer, as independent as the savage land which gave her birth. At her French debut in *Le Diable Boiteux*, it was said that her little legs could take Taglioni-length strides and that in three leaps she covered the stage from back to front. Her elevation, her *entrechats*, her over-all skill in matters of virtuosity were like those of a man.

The French, public and critics, admired her extravagantly, but by their frequent comments upon her strength and remarkable agility and thrusting leaps, it was apparent that they sensed a touch of acrobatics. This personal, perhaps racial way of dance would disturb Europeans as often as an American ballerina performed in their lands. In the mid-twentieth century (especially in England), they would carp about the acrobatic, the athletic nature of the American dancer, blind to the fact that the American dance artist is neither a professional acrobat nor a professional athlete but the product of a land in which physical strength, energy, competition, and space-covering speed constitute a national heritage. When Karen Conrad, on the occasion of the first performance by Ballet Theatre a century after Augusta made her Paris debut, leaped skywards in *Les Sylphides*, covering the stage diagonally in three leaps (or so the legend runs), she was not purposely athletic or acrobatic. It was perfectly natural for a sylph from Philadelphia to leap that high. For another and earlier Philadelphian, Augusta Maywood, such actions were also natural.

The little Augusta also succeeded in creating other sensations. She eloped at the close of one performance at the Opéra with a dancer, Mabille, and, as a minor, had to be dragged back to Paris. This episode did not sit well with prudish Americans, nor did her refusal to return to her native land. In addition, her treatment of her family in later years caused distress, for although she apparently contributed to their support from time to time, their declining years were supposedly passed in poverty. But, above everything, Maywood loved to dance, and although she never returned to America, she gave America something to be proud of, artistically if not morally.

The birth of a baby presumably caused a brief lull in her career, but soon she was ready to perform again, this time in new regions. For three years she enchanted the Portuguese, who found her "incomparable" in *Giselle* and other ballets. Vienna, too, loved her, and Maywood, completely unafraid of competition, danced with

AUGUSTA MAYWOOD

Europe's leading stars and, furthermore, saw to it that she received equal billing. In 1848, she went to Italy, the country which was to become her home and the scene of her greatest successes.

Together with Elssler, who apparently was her friend, she shared the grandiose title of *prima ballerina e prima mima assoluta* at La Scala. With the best male dancers as her partners, she formed a company with toured Italy in presentations of ballets made famous by Taglioni, Elssler, Grisi, Grahn, and Cerito, in newly choreographed Italian ballets, and, interestingly enough, in a ballet version of *Uncle Tom's Cabin*. Her final success was in a ballet based upon the story of Camille, and this highly dramatic piece served her until her retirement in 1862, when, as had happened to Grahn earlier in England, opera commenced to displace the art of dancing.

Mary Ann Lee, 1823–1847?, born and trained in Philadelphia, was a contemporary and rival of Maywood. She not only did some choreography but also imported to America ballets popular in Europe. She performed many of Fanny Elssler's solos, and following a brief period of study in Paris with the choreographer of Giselle, she was able to present America with its very first Giselle. Retired in 1847.

The little Augusta had had only one American rival, Mary Ann Lee of Philadelphia. Mary Ann, who had made her debut at the same time as the little Augusta and in the same ballet, was never her rival's equal, but in America she won wide fame for herself as a classic ballerina. But where Augusta's life was comparatively easy, apparently happy, and always successful, Mary Ann faced hardships and tragedy in her quest for fame.

MARY ANN LEE IN
"LA JOLIE FILLE DE GAND"

Her father, an acrobat (her mother was a dancer), died when Mary Ann was a child, and to help support the family she performed on every possible occasion. She acted, she did fancy dances, she took supporting roles in ballets, she danced in a very unlikely version of *La Sylphide*, and she managed to learn the famous role of Cachucha from Elssler's partner. In 1838, when she was only fifteen, a ballet, *The Lily Queen*, was created especially for her, and the following year she made her New York debut. Pretty and sprightly, she won the plaudits of the public and was commended for what would seem to us the distinctly odd ability of "reclining into *attitudes* at the end of every strain!"

A year of study, of touring, of performing for P. T. Barnum of circus fame saw her developing into an accomplished dancer, almost a ballerina. By 1840, she had mastered almost all of Elssler's solos, appeared in full-length ballets, sung as well as danced, tried her hand at choreography, had the experience of a really long tour, and frolicked in a burlesque of *La Bayadère* (or *The Maid of Cashmere*), which was impudently named *Buy It Dear, 'Tis Made of Cashmere*.

By 1844, Mary Ann Lee had enough money set aside to travel to Paris, where she studied with Coralli, choreographer of *Giselle*, at the Académie (although she never appeared at the Opéra) and learned from him the choreographies of *Giselle*, *La Jolie Fille de Gand*, and *La Fille du Danube*. Thus, upon her return, Mary Ann Lee, American ballerina, was able to mount and present to America its first *Giselle*. This she did in Boston with George Washington Smith, the first American *premier danseur noble* (classic male dancer), as her partner. Mme. Augusta, a French dancer in no way related to the little Augusta, beat Mary Ann with the New York

94

première of *Giselle*, but the first American ballerina was not long in presenting her authoritative version to New York and to the nation.

With the little Augusta gone and with Julia Turnbull, an actress turned dancer, as her nearest rival, Mary Ann Lee was supreme in her post as the top American-born ballerina. But tragedy struck before her career was barely under way. While she was on tour with her company, her health commenced to fail, and at twenty-four she was forced to retire from the stage. She did make infrequent appearances from time to time, but the fame and fortune of this early American ballerina were irrevocably halted. Would she have gone on to greater success? Would she have joined Maywood in an American conquest of Europe? One cannot say. But if Lafontaine had been the first of the first ballerinas and Maywood had been the first of the American ballerinas to win international fame, Mary Ann Lee became America's own, first classic ballerina, a worthy ancestress to the Tallchiefs and the Kayes of today.

But except for Lee, Maywood, and Turnbull, America produced no true ballerinas during the nineteenth century. Stars and troupes from other lands took charge of America's ballet culture and even the resident opera associations turned to Europe for their ballerinas and their ballets. Indigenous artists and indigenous ideas were few, but the teachers, many of them celebrated visitors who remained when their performing days were over, kept busy training young Americans for that still distant day when the word "ballerina" could have the word "American" in front of it.

Marie Bonfanti, 1851–1921. An Italian ballerina famous for her appearance in "The Black Crook," a musical extravaganza produced in New York in 1866.

THE BLACK CROOK

MARIE BONFANTI

Of the scores of imported ballerinas who came to America to dance and to teach, a typical example was Marie Bonfanti, ballerina of the Paris Opéra and of Covent Garden. Her vehicle was one of the most spectacular productions America had ever seen, *The Black Crook*, which ran for almost two years (1866 was the opening year) in New York, which spawned touring companies, and which paved the way for endless extravaganzas. A major ingredient in this mammoth spectacle was ballet and the star was Bonfanti. Assisted by another ballerina (Rita Sangalli), a bevy of top soloists (both male and female), and fifty "auxiliary ladies," Bonfanti led the way to public acclaim through extremely inferior drama, gorgeous settings, and vistas peopled with nymphs and demons.

Since the ballet proved to be the most popular part of this bright and gaudy theatrical mess, it provided dancing in America with another brief period of popularity. Bonfanti, light and graceful and highly accomplished, was warmly welcomed and managed to survive the nearly six hours it required to present the opening performance of *The Black Crook*. Once this uncouth, nineteenth-century answer to *Le Ballet Comique de la Reine* had run its happy, entertaining course and it and its successors had been subjected to violent criticisms from pulpits and friendly attacks by multitudes storming the box-offices, Bonfanti settled down to teach.

As a ballet teacher in America, Bonfanti doubtless enjoyed considerable prestige and success, but one of her most famous pupils failed, at the time, to make the grade. "After I learned three of the possible five positions," she later reported, "Madame asked me to leave the class. I never returned." The youngster, who didn't actually want to be a ballet dancer at all, went on to become one of the greatest (and perhaps the greatest) non-ballet dancer the world had

98

ever seen. Her name was Ruth St. Denis.

But where was the American ballerina during the span of a century? She was Mary Ann Lee, finished at twenty-four. She was Augusta Maywood, dancing abroad. She was also, quite possibly, a hundred other girls who never had a chance to win the coveted title. Patently, America could have produced at least one great ballerina and many others of ballerina caliber during the generations which elapsed between Mary Ann's untimely retirement and the birth of American ballet in the twentieth century. But America did not.

In the nineteenth century, the time had not come when ballet was to be recognized as an international art form, a technique of movement belonging to all nations and accepting, even requiring, the colorings which each race and nation and region could bring to it. The potential American ballerina, because no one would give her a chance, had to wait, hidden safely away in a *corps de ballet* where she could not shine, where the vigor of her dancing could not possibly rival the polished behavior of a European star. Europe wanted it that way, America wanted it that way. Only some unknown, unsung American girl may have believed differently, but she would have been ahead of her times, way, way ahead, for an American girl with ballerina ambitions was doomed to disappointment until long after the twentieth century had begun.

VIRGINIA ZUCCHI

RUSSIAN BALLERINA

Virginia Zucchi, 1847–1930, Italian ballerina, who reinvigorated ballet in Russia through her introduction of virtuoso Italian technique into the Russian Imperial Ballet, theretofore an employer of the gentler French technique of ballet. Her fine technique, her physical daring, and her great acting skill inspired Petipa, the choreographer, and had the Russian public at her feet.

The Russian ballerina—her name, until very recently, synonymous with stardom in dance—had almost as difficult a time as her unheralded American sister. In the nineteenth century she, too, had to make way for importations and bow to the supposed superiority of ballerinas from the Paris Opéra or from the opera houses of Italy. Two native Russian artists, however, rose to the status of ballerina. They were Elena Andreyanova, who specialized in Taglioni roles, and the almost legendary Istomina. But these two, contemporaries of Taglioni, were pitted against a legion of visiting celebrities. The Russian ballerina's time had not yet come.

Everywhere, in the middle and late nineteenth century, opera was making advances, artistically and in popularity, while ballet was either standing still (a silly state of affairs for the art of movement) or dying. There were, of course, ballet performances throughout Europe and there were ballet stars, but both had become secondary to the art and artists of music.

In Russia, things were almost as bad. There were dance perform-

101

ances but only the unreconstructed dance fans seemed to care. That is, until Virginia Zucchi came out of Italy to give Russian ballet a much needed shot of energy. Zucchi, a product of those great Italian ballet schools which, in that century, were supplying the world with its finest teachers and greatest ballerinas, changed the course of Russian ballet. The soft and graceful French style of dance which had prevailed in the Imperial School and Theater ended with Zucchi, who introduced, in 1885, the brilliant, sharp technique of the Italians and something of Italy's fire.

Zucchi, who had been born in 1847, had been a pupil of the great Italian teacher, Carlo Blasis, and had risen from the *corps* to ballerina status at the opera in Padua. As a guest artist, she had also experienced considerable success in opera-ballet appearances elsewhere in her native land and in Madrid, Berlin, Paris, and London. Her actual St. Petersburg debut was modest, for she had been engaged to appear on the nineteenth-century equivalent of the "straw-hat" or "subway" circuit, that is to say, in a summer theater. But so successful was she that the Imperial Ballet signed her immediately for one season and she remained for seven years.

In Zucchi, the power of the ballerina was epitomized. Alone, she changed the dance style of the Russian nation. Alone, she triumphed over routine material to draw the public back to ballet. The great choreographer needs a great ballerina to breathe life into his works, and when there are no great choreographies, it is the ballerina, the star personality, whose task it is to keep the art alive through performing alone. Zucchi was the symbol of this ballet essential, the ballerina. She had the Russian public at her feet and the jewels of adoring aristocrats about her neck.

And how Zucchi must have danced! She executed daring and

dangerous movements with effortless grace. She put soul and fire and belief into her characterizations. Not for her the impeccable behavior of the French dancer. If the role called for frenzy, Zucchi delivered with flashing feet and wild eyes, with dress ripped and hair awry. Zucchi was an actress, one of the finest actress-dancers in the annals of ballet, and while the art was sinking toward its theatrical nadir in France, England, and even Italy, she was driving it toward a new zenith in Russia.

Elevation was not her forte—she was a *terre à terre* dancer—but her technique was powerful, her manner energetic, her mime supreme, and her personality vivid. Marius Petipa, the Imperial Theater's ballet master and immortal choreographer, must have worshipped Zucchi. They quarreled happily, but here was someone who could invest dancing with new vigor, here was an inspiring artist, here was a personality who could aid him in the renewal of classical ballet. Here was the first of a series of real stars with whom Petipa would unite his genius to create an unforgettable era in ballet.

When Zucchi departed from Russia in 1892 for European tours and eventual retirement in Monte Carlo as head of her own school, she left behind her a new style of Russian ballet (Italian but capable of being absorbed) and influences upon Benois (to become a top designer), Kchessinskaya (to become the first of the modern Russian ballerinas), and innumerable other young artists of the Russian dance theater. She also left behind her the vision of the individual triumphing over the art conditions of her time.

PIERINA LEGNANI

Pierina Legnani, 1863–1923, Italian ballerina who, along with Zucchi, was responsible for the change of ballet style in Russia. Legnani, who had been prima ballerina assoluta *in Milan, made her Russian debut in 1893. An amazing virtuoso, she was the first to execute the sequence of thirty-two* fouettés. *In 1895, she created the role of Queen of the Swans in the St. Petersburg version of* Swan Lake.

No sooner had Zucchi departed than Pierina Legnani arrived. If the first Italian had made the Russians conscious of a new style of ballet dancing, the second Italian made them doubly aware of technical virtuosity. She, too, had come from Italy, where she had been *prima ballerina assoluta* at Milan, and from successes in Paris, Madrid, and London. Her Russian debut in 1893 (when she was just thirty) at St. Petersburg in *Cinderella* was nothing short of fantastic. It was then that the balletomane commenced counting *pirouettes*, measuring leg extensions, and timing balances, for Legnani brought to Russian ballet the pyrotechnics associated with the coloratura soprano. If the public wanted extreme virtuosity and found it in the operatic voice, Legnani was the girl to convince them that virtuosity of the muscles was even more exciting.

With her creation of the role of Swan Queen in the St. Petersburg staging of *Swan Lake* in 1895 (an earlier Moscow version had been a dismal failure), Legnani's career in Russia and her place in history were secure. She had come to the Imperial Ballet for a single season, but, like Zucchi, she had not been permitted to leave until seven years had passed.

To Legnani, the dance world owes the ever-exciting miracle of the multiple (very multiple) *fouetté*, for Legnani was the first to accomplish thirty-two of these whipping turns in sequence. When she sprang this feat upon the Russian public, an ecstatic audience applauded so enthusiastically that there was nothing for Legnani to do but repeat the variation and this she did to bravos which have echoed down the years. For many, many seasons, these *fouettés* and other examples of physical virtuosity would remain the exclusive property of the few until the coming of a new and bustling ballet era in the 1930's, when thirty-two or even sixty-four *fouettés* would be a part of the dance vocabulary of almost every advanced student.

Mathilde Kchessinskaya, born 1872, the first Russian-born ballerina to match the virtuosity of the Italian ballerinas. With Kchessinskaya, the only Russian to receive the title prima ballerina assoluta, *the period of Russian-ballerina supremacy was launched. Kchessinskaya, still living, is teaching in Paris.*

Zucchi and Legnani, both of whom died not so very long ago, lived to see the eclipse of the Italian ballerina and the rise of the Russian dance star. Even before Legnani had left the Imperial Ballet, two native ballerinas, Olga Preobrajenska and Mathilde Kchessinskaya, had risen to stardom. For more than a quarter of a century, Preobrajenska danced on the Imperial stage. As a *prima ballerina,* she was seen and admired and loved in *Giselle, Coppélia, The Sleeping Beauty, Nutcracker,* and countless other ballets, and she was surpassed, officially at any rate, by one other artist, Kchessinskaya, the first, last, and only Russian to receive the title (granted by the Imperial Court) of *prima ballerina assoluta.*

CATHERINE GELTZER

MATHILDE KCHESSINSKAYA
IN "LA ESMERALDA"

OLGA PREOBRAJENSKA
IN "COPPÉLIA"

Kchessinskaya, tiny and light, meticulous in movement and an extraordinary technician, discovered for herself Legnani's secret of virtuosity. Neither Preobrajenska nor even the younger Karsavina and Pavlova could or would attempt the thirty-two *fouettés* and the like, and so it was left to Kchessinskaya to make the Russian ballerina a figure without equal in the realm of dance virtuosity. Her achievements, then, were a source of national pride, for she had wrested the ballerina's crown of laurel from French, Italian, and Scandinavian heads and placed it firmly on a Russian brow.

As the wife of a Grand Duke, she came to know the Czar himself, and access to the royal ear enabled her to wield enormous power in the ballet. She was in a position to help a young dancer named Vaslav Nijinsky along the way to success, but this same loftiness of position made it necessary for her to flee Russia at the outbreak of the Revolution.

Olga Preobrajenska, born 1871, Russian ballerina and contemporary of Kchessinskaya. Together, the two exemplified the accomplishments of the Russian dance star. Preobrajenska, numbering several of the leading modern ballerinas among her pupils, teaches in Paris.

With Preobrajenska and Kchessinskaya, Russia was, at last, satisfied. For a time, the dance world outside of Russia knew of these two great stars, of Egorova, Trefilova, Geltzer, Spessivtzeva, the slightly younger Pavlova and Karsavina, and others only by hearsay. But the center of ballet had obviously shifted to the land of the Russians and soon, from that center, would come Russian ballerinas, Russian companies, and Russian teachers to make the term "Russian ballet" tantamount to the term "ballet" throughout the world.

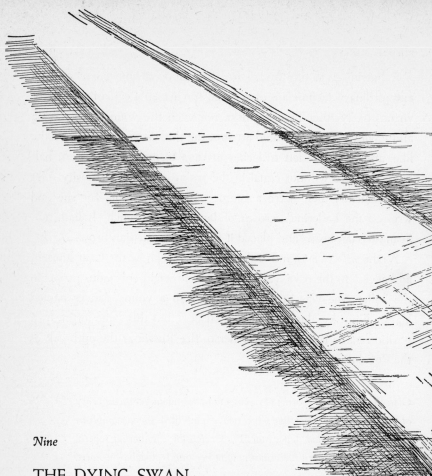

Nine

THE DYING SWAN

Anna Pavlova, 1881–1931, Russian ballerina who became the most famous ballerina in the world, danced The Dying Swan *solo for the first time in 1905 and became a prima ballerina in 1906. In 1910, she made her first appearance in the United States in New York at the Metropolitan Opera House in Coppélia. Her tours took her all over the world, to towns and villages as well as to cities. To millions, Pavlova was ballet itself. She never retired. She died of pneumonia while on tour.*

112

ANNA PAVLOVA IN "THE DYING SWAN"

It was the anniversary of a death. The curtain rose on the empty stage of a Broadway theater. But was it empty? A light explored, ever so gently, the patterns of a dance as if in search of the dancer. And the sad, sweet music played on. The stage was empty but the hearts of many New Yorkers in the year 1941 were filled with memories—even though ten years had passed—of a divine dancer, of Anna Pavlova, whose *Dying Swan* had meant ballet itself to almost all the world.

A decade earlier, in Brussels, the same mournful tribute had been paid, for Pavlova had just died. But the scheduled performance went on without the star. The company danced and an imaginary Pavlova seemed to be moving just beyond the range of a spotlight which sought its subject in vain. The year was 1931. Two years before, Serge Diaghilev, the great Russian impresario who had brought great dancers and great artistic ideas out of Russia to create new "Ballets Russes" for audiences in Western Europe and America, had died; a later Ballet Russe, stemming from Diaghilev's accomplishments, had yet to be born; a curtain was already descending slowly between Russia's state ballet and the rest of the world. With Pavlova's passing, it seemed that ballet, too, had died.

Fifty years before, a premature and frail baby had been born into a humble and exceeding poor family. The simple St. Petersburg home witnessed the death of the father when Anna was only two, witnessed a series of illnesses which racked the already frail body of the child, and witnessed, too, the piety and the labor of a devoted mother and the first dreams of a career which was to extend the art of ballet to every quarter of the globe.

One day, a very special treat was arranged for little Anna. She was taken to see the Imperial Ballet in a performance of *The Sleep-*

ing Beauty. To the wide-eyed girl, everything seemed captivating, from the enormous theater itself to the color of a costume, from the shining ballerina to the most obscure member of the vast company of performers.

Here, at the ballet, Anna found a fairy tale come to life as a lovely Princess and her Prince Charming, an evil witch and good fairies danced a story of enchantment. Scenes of castles and of magic forests thrilled her, and Tchaikovsky's beautiful music for the ballet made her wish to dance herself. But most exciting of all was the ballerina. She was beautiful, she was radiant, she was gracious, and she moved so exquisitely across the ground and through the air that she seemed, to the child, a real Princess.

The eight-year-old Anna, watching the ballerina and the wonderful world of the theater, knew at that moment the course of her own life. If the child had been a twentieth-century American school girl, she would have said, "That's for me." Anna said the equivalent to her disbelieving mother and meant it.

Two years later, she passed all the necessary entrance examinations and was admitted to the Imperial School of Ballet. Her life had begun, and it was a life for which great things were predicted. From the start she excelled, not only in dancing but also in her other subjects, and when graduation time came in 1899, she was placed, not in the *corps de ballet*, but one rank higher, among the select group of *coryphées*. Since rank in ballet was almost as strict as that of the military, it may be said that Anna Pavlova never served as a buck private. She commenced her service as a corporal or, at the very least, as a private first class.

Quickly she rose from *coryphée* to second soloist, then to first soloist, and, in 1905, to ballerina. The following year, she passed that test of tests, *Swan Lake,* and became a *prima ballerina* of the Russian Imperial Ballet. During her first decade as a dancer of the Imperial Theater, all sorts of important events had occurred in her life. She had, of course, fulfilled her vow to become Princess Aurora in *The Sleeping Beauty* and she had also danced *Giselle* (both the title role and the Wili queen), the old *La Bayadère, Don Quixote, Paquita,* and practically all the standard repertory.

It was in this period—1905 to be exact—that a young and rebellious choreographer agreed to create a solo for the new ballerina and, in what legend reports was roughly an hour, Michel Fokine composed *The Dying Swan.* It was, for its time, a revolutionary piece, for in defiance of the virtuoso fashion established by Zucchi and Legnani and triumphantly continued by Kchessinskaya and others, the new solo was not a show-off piece. It was a simple dance, so simple that thousands upon thousands of ballet students would one day attempt to imitate it (and unsuccessfully). It suited Pavlova just as it would have appealed to Taglioni because it was romantic, because it required genius to capture its elusive magic.

Yet another important event took place during this decade. Pavlova, in 1907, commenced her first dancing travels beyond the borders of her homeland. The northern nations saw her first, and in Stockholm the worshiping crowds escorted her from the theater to her hotel and the King honored her with a decoration. Next came the central European countries and then Paris (with the new Russian company headed by the ambitious Serge Diaghilev), the southern lands of Spain and Italy, and finally a return to France and the Paris Opéra itself.

Her link with Taglioni was growing stronger. Among her teachers was Christian Johannsen, who had actually danced with Taglioni;

The Dying Swan, with its purity and gentleness, had brought her even closer; and now the tours, inspired by Taglioni's example, were coming to spread a dance message far and wide. She continued to dance in her home theater until 1913 (when she left Russia never to return) but the travels were becoming increasingly important to her and ever broader in scope. England, America, the whole world were to be hers. Russia was not enough, nor was Paris, where all eyes were focused upon the mighty events generated by Serge Diaghilev and the new expatriate Russian ballet.

At first it seemed that Pavlova's destiny would be inseparable from that of the new ballet order. In Russia, Fokine had created several ballets for her and she appeared to be in sympathy not only with the aims of the young choreographer but also with Diaghilev's plans. She did make appearances with the Diaghilev troupe, dancing, among other ballets, *Les Sylphides* with Nijinsky and Tamara Karsavina, but for many reasons she refused to become a permanent fixture. Pavlova, unlike Augusta Maywood, was not given to seeking out competition and Nijinsky was a formidable rival in any company. Furthermore, in spite of her association with Fokine, she was pretty much of a conventionalist and the new company's new productions were, perhaps, too revolutionary for her tastes or unsuited to her special talent.

The explanation for her unwillingness to be associated with this organization permanently lay, it may be presumed, in her great personal ambition. She was not against either different styles of dance or innovations, as attested by her admiration for Isadora Duncan and her keen interest in and approval of the methods and discoveries of Jacques Dalcroze, Mary Wigman, and others. When she first saw Princess Aurora, Pavlova's ambition was clear, and when she became Princess Aurora, she was free to do exactly as she pleased. No one was to rival her. No one was to interfere with her desire to spread beauty and happiness in bands of dance around the earth.

When Pavlova, with Mikhail Mordkin as her virile and accomplished partner, made her New York debut at the Metropolitan Opera House in 1910, she inaugurated a new era of ballet in America. The winsome Danish ballerina, Adeline Genée, had won thousands of admirers; Isadora Duncan and Ruth St. Denis were fighting successfully and gloriously for the establishment of new concepts of dance; Bonfanti was an exciting memory in the hearts of many grandparents; but nothing to touch the personality and the performing sorcery of Pavlova had been imported from Europe to America since Fanny Elssler had caused the Congress of the United States to adjourn.

She made her American debut in *Coppélia*, the story of a mischievous girl who pretends to be a doll and wreaks all sorts of delightful havoc in a toy shop. For the initial season, Pavlova and Mordkin were supported by the Metropolitan Opera's not very accomplished *corps* in those of their presentations which required a company. But later, in England, a permanent ensemble was formed, thus making it possible for Pavlova to establish a repertory suitable for any occasion, for any theater from a school auditorium to the great old Hippodrome itself.

World War I deprived Europe of Pavlova and Pavlova of her home, Ivy House, in England. But what the Old World lost, the New World gained, and for five years the ballerina and her company toured the Americas, North, Central, and South. It was not easy. The average of two performances a week at the Imperial Theater was changed to read seven or eight or more in America. The fragile-appearing ballerina, however, was made of something very like steel. She was enduring, untiring, indestructible. Not even a half-year stint at New York's mammoth house of spectacles, the Hippodrome, could dampen her ardor for performing. And her tours to almost every city, village, and town in the United States brought glimpses of fairyland to hundreds of thousands who had never seen ballet before and thousands who would probably never see it again, as well as satisfaction to an ambitious, dedicated priestess of dance beauty.

At the close of the war, Pavlova commenced those unceasing travels which were to take her and, with her, ballet into the lives of millions in Egypt, Burma, South Africa, Malay, Costa Rica, Australia, Java, everywhere. Hundreds of thousands of miles, thousands of performances, millions of onlookers—these constituted her service to ballet, her own justification for being. For Pavlova's greatest contribution to the art of dance was . . . Anna Pavlova. Many dance scholars found her generally undistinguished, her settings and costumes inferior, much of her music doggerel, and the majority of her ballets and dances trite and insubstantial; but all agreed that Pavlova, the ballerina and messenger, was triumphant.

Of course she continued to dance *Giselle* and *Coppélia* and a few other masterpieces, but her repertory consisted mainly of variations from the old ballets and new pieces in a vein which recalled the pixies and sprites of a much earlier day—*Autumn Leaves*, *Dragonfly*, *Snowflakes*, and *California Poppy*. There was not much in the way of thematic meatiness in those. There were others: *The Dying Swan*, naturally, and *Gavotte*, little solos, duets, *divertissements*, and ballets, some with folk flavors and others classically Romantic.

Her own choreography and the creations of others who composed for her had no effect at all upon those who would later build an American ballet. But Pavlova rose above her material to make the world conscious of a very special art and to inspire countless children, as she herself had been inspired, to make dancing a career. Her mere presence upon a stage roused the dance passion in an Agnes de Mille and in unnamed and unknown youngsters across America. Because of her, ballet schools and their enrollments multiplied, and because of her pioneering, new pathways were opened to the ballet performers and companies who would follow.

Faults galore may be found in her. Not only did she present inferior dance materials on the stage, but her very form of dance was dead, long dead, except for the miracle of her performing. She avoided competition and she discarded partners so frequently—because of incompatibility, the personal ambitions of the male, or her own solo ambitiousness—that the only artistic permanence in her company was herself. She worked incredibly hard, never coddling herself, always critical of Pavlova, yet she tended to avoid demanding roles in major creations, roles in which she might conceivably invite comparisons with other ballerinas.

She was not a virtuoso. She did possess a remarkable balance but thirty-two *fouettés* were not for her nor, as a matter of fact, were multiple *pirouettes*. Yet Pavlova was the unofficial *prima ballerina assoluta* of the world. In *The Dying Swan*, she did little more than *bourrée* about the stage, fluttering her arms and hands, curving her lovely neck, permitting a tremor to ripple through her body, and it was the greatest dancing anyone had ever seen.

It mattered not at all what Pavlova danced. It was how she danced that made her the idol of millions, the symbol of ballet. Words which had been used to describe Taglioni were revived for

Anna Pavlova. She was light of motion, airy, effortless, yet a spiritual ecstasy seemed to pervade her being, sending forth its radiant power to touch everyone present. With her the old was reborn and repetitions were new. Perfection was hers, perfection of foot and leg, perfection in a sort of sad beauty, perfection of balletic line, perfection in the communication of that ecstatic conviction which is the heart of art.

In spite of her faults in taste and in artistic judgment, in spite of the mediocrity which surrounded her almost always, Pavlova the ballerina was perfect, the most perfect and powerful individual force that the ballet had ever, in its four hundred years of effort, produced. And yet when this winged one of the theater was dying, she was still unsatisfied with herself, still certain that her mission for ballet was unfinished; mortally ill with pneumonia, her last request was to her maid to prepare her swan costume. The show went on, but without Pavlova. Only a light remained.

TAMARA KARSAVINA IN "LES SYLPHIDES"

Tamara Karsavina, born 1885, Russian ballerina and contemporary of Pavlova. She is most famous for her association with Serge Diaghilev and the Russian ballet which he took to Western Europe in 1909. She created many roles in new ballets by Fokine, Massine, and others, and through these parts she was able to inaugurate a new type of ballerina, one who was a technician, an actress, a stylist, and an artist of the lyric theater. Now in retirement, she lives in England.

Pavlova had no rivals but she did have contemporaries. Among them was Tamara Karsavina, without whom Diaghilev and Fokine might have failed in their initial enterprise in bringing a new Russian ballet to the West.

Karsavina, too, was Russian-born but, unlike Pavlova, she came of a family of artists and her entry into the Imperial Ballet School—since she was the gifted daughter of a distinguished dancer—was practically predestined. The young beauty made her debut with the Imperial company in 1902. Although she danced, as ballerina, principal roles in the usual *Swan Lake, Nutcracker, Giselle, The Sleeping Beauty*, and the like, she was not granted the title of *prima ballerina* until after she had made her name a household word in Paris as a star of the Diaghilev company.

In spite of her status at home and her enthusiasm, which she shared with Fokine and Pavlova, for Diaghilev's plans for the future of Russian ballet, she was not engaged as a ballerina for the first (1909) season in Paris. Hers were to be the secondary roles, the first going to Kchessinskaya and Pavlova. But Kchessinskaya suddenly backed out of the venture (although she did make some appearances with the company), Pavlova soon went on to solo ventures, and a third ballerina faded from the picture. Only Karsavina was left, and the strangely neglectful Diaghilev and Fokine quickly transformed her into their ballerina.

Karsavina created ballerina roles in almost all of Fokine's early and vastly important works. She danced in *Les Sylphides* (with Pavlova and Nijinsky), *Carnaval, Petrouchka, Le Spectre de la Rose, Firebird* (title role), *Thamar* (title role), *Daphnis and Chloë,* and *Coq d'Or*, as well as in Massine's *The Three-Cornered Hat*. More difficult, she had to dance with Nijinsky, the most sensational male dancer of the age, and still try to retain and communicate the power of the ballerina.

With becoming modesty, co-operativeness, and consummate skill, Karsavina accomplished everything expected of her. She was considered the finest exponent of Fokine's modern style of ballet and yet she continued to be a classic ballerina of the highest order. She danced on the stage with Nijinsky, yet the audience did not forget Karsavina. Classical, *demi-caractère*, and character assignments were equally easy for an artist who possessed nobility of bearing, poetry of movement, mastery of period styles, and dramatic sensitivity.

America saw her only once, and then in an unsatisfactory concert presentation, but Karsavina belonged to the great companies and her beauty required the glittering frame of the opera-house stage. Now, in happy retirement in England, she can look back upon a career which was as important as that of Anna Pavlova, although far less spectacular. One, in isolated splendor, served up immortal dance in very mortal containers. The other, uniting with fellow artists, helped to build a ballet structure which would welcome and protect both the art and the artist for years to come. Pavlova left a light to guide the dreaming, hoping dance initiate. Karsavina, as ballerina of a great company and exponent of a new order in ballet, bequeathed a model of the dancer-actress-technician-stylist, the star of the lyric ballet theater of the future.

THE BABY BALLERINAS

Tamara Toumanova, one of the Russian-born "baby ballerinas" of the 1930's. Of the three she is the most famous, since she has continued an active dance career as star or guest star of many of the world's leading ballet organizations. Early in her career, Balanchine created Cotillon and La Concurrence especially for her, and she has distinguished herself also in Firebird, in the "Black Swan" pas de deux, as Princess Aurora, and, particularly, as the Beloved in Massine's Symphonie Fantastique.

TAMARA TOUMANOVA
IN "LE TRICORNE"

It was a command performance for the King and Queen of England. Naturally, the young dancer, a ballerina in her teens, was excited, eager to display her virtuosity. The musical cue for the variation almost entirely composed of *grands jetés* came and the youngster commenced those leaps in *Les Sylphides* which slash across the stage in strong diagonal lines. But she got no further than her initial movement, for so energetic was she that in mid-air she turned upside down and landed on her head. Irina Baronova, baby ballerina, was knocked out cold, and another baby ballerina, Tatiana Riabouchinska, stepped (or leaped) in and finished the variation for Their Majesties. So goes the story that Baronova tells on herself.

The falling on the head was a comparatively unusual event, but what, one may ask, was so unusual about a teen-age ballerina's dancing for royalty? The truth of the matter is that teen-age ballerinas were rare in the early 1930's. Long since forgotten were the ballerinas of the Romantic age of ballet, and the stars of the Diaghilev company, which had launched the great revival of ballet interest in Western Europe and in America, were young adults. The public was accustomed to youth in ballet and was understandably delighted when a teen-age prodigy assumed ballerina roles, but to come upon a trio of ballerinas—Baronova, Riabouchinska, and Tamara Toumanova—still on the edge of childhood was indeed a novel experience.

But all three of the baby ballerinas were energetic virtuosos, equipped to accomplish any physical feat tossed their way. They represented not only a young generation but a new generation of Russian dancers. For them, those technical tricks which Italian ballerinas had brought to Russia, thereby embarrassing all the Russian ballerinas with the exception of the determined Kchessinskaya, were

128

no trouble at all. Multiple *fouettés*? Why stop at thirty-two? Why not sixty-four or more? The traditions of Russian ballet were theirs, but in addition they had experienced harsh and demanding childhoods and they were thrown into a balletic era in which both traditionalism and experimentation called for dancers willing and able to dance almost anything.

Diaghilev was dead and the first great swell of international interest in ballet seemed to have subsided. Furthermore, Russian and Russian-trained dancers of the great impresario's organization had scattered. No one was quite certain just what the formula of recovery would be. Perhaps Massine or Balanchine, distinguished and imaginative choreographers, could swing the trick, but who would be the dancers or, more specifically, the ballerinas? Something new, something startling seemed to be in order, so with the establishment by René Blum and Colonel W. de Basil of the Ballet Russe de Monte Carlo in 1932, the baby ballerinas were born. Officially, Alexandra Danilova was the ballerina, but publicity tactics centered around the babies, Barnova, Toumanova, and Riabouchinska.

The three had been born in Russia during the Revolution. Toumanova actually had been born in a boxcar as the train, traveling across the wastes of Siberia, bore her White Russian parents away from the turmoils and dangers of their native St. Petersburg. The year was 1919 and another baby ballerina was born, not in flight but in St. Petersburg (or Petrograd, now Leningrad) itself, and a year would pass before Barnova, her mother, and her navy-officer father would seek sanctuary outside their native land. The third, a Moscow baby, was Riabouchinska.

Eventually, the little girls and their families arrived in Paris and the three children commenced their studies with Olga Preobrajenska,

129

onetime *prima ballerina* of the Imperial Ballet. Toumanova was the first to make her debut. At the age of seven, she appeared in concert with Pavlova, and by the time she was a veteran of eleven, she was prepared to perform in a children's ballet at the Paris Opéra. In between these two major events, appearances at parties and entertainments kept her occupied. But the real chance came when Balanchine, scouting for artists for the new Ballet Russe and for his own independent ventures, discovered in Preobrajenska's studio both Toumanova and Baronova. When Riabouchinska joined them, the history-making trio was completed.

The oldsters shook their heads at such precocity. Surely, the three were being forced like hothouse plants. They would flower quickly and die (artistically) young. Another point: how could children be expected to discover and define the many important details of a role? The old-timers were, for the most part, wrong. The hard training and the much harder performing did not injure the young ladies and they commenced to grow as artists.

But at first, youth and physical skill were paramount. When they made their formal debuts with the De Basil company, they were hardly into adolescence, yet principal roles were entrusted to them, new ballets were created for them, and the producers gambled the future of the company upon their popularity. It worked, for not only Europe but also America, commencing with the first of the annual tours in 1933, took the babies to their hearts. In the immediate past, children of their age would still have been in ballet school or, at the most, in the *corps de ballet* (probably as supernumeraries or participants in children's performances) of the Imperial Theater; yet here were Baronova, Toumanova, and Riabouchinska, teen-age stars of the dance.

130

Toumanova, always burdened by such appelations as "the black pearl of Russia," "the black swan," or the black this or that, was the most glittering of the three. Her black hair, dark eyes, high cheekbones, and generous mouth provided her with the elements of instant visual projection. In addition, she possessed (and still does) a technical equipment which enabled her to do almost anything. Multiple turns, long balances, tricks old and new bothered her not at all. By the time she was fifteen or sixteen, she had apparently mastered nearly everything the classroom had to offer in the way of purely physical accomplishment and commenced to be concerned about artistry: the smooth fusing of steps and sequences of movement, the delineation of character, the mastery of style.

In her quest of artistry, Toumanova was partly successful. To certain parts she brought ease of movement, tenderness, delicacy, and a haunting romanticism, but in other roles, especially those which offered opportunities for virtuosity, she tended, some critics felt, to oversell herself and her technique. She hammed (audiences were heard to snicker), perhaps not intentionally, but she seemed to comment upon her own skill at balancing on point for endless periods, upon the dizzying speed of her pirouettes, upon the circus ingredients of dancing. If anything, she needed to underplay, such was the natural vividness of her presence.

For her, in the first days of the Ballet Russe, Balanchine created *Cotillon* and *La Concurrence*, and with these Toumanova became a star of a new ballet order. Later, when she joined Balanchine's own company, Les Ballets 1933, *Mozartiana*, *Le Bourgeois Gentilhomme*, and *Songes* were added to her growing repertory. Of all her roles in contemporary ballets, perhaps the one which enchanted Americans most was that of the Beloved in Massine's *Symphonie*

131

Fantastique (Berlioz). Here, not only her technical range but also her lyrical and dramatic gifts were exploited. She was incredibly lovely, elusive, desirable as the heroine, and in the nightmarish closing passages of the ballet a terrifyingly macabre element was introduced, permitting the ballerina to reveal her tremendous dynamic force which, when properly channeled, served the cause of dramatic art.

No one, however, can forget her performances in the "Black Swan" *pas de deux* or in *Aurora's Wedding*. In the former, she has been inclined to exaggerate everything, but one cannot deny the excitement of her flashing *fouettés*, the steely balances, the miraculous speed which never interferes with meticulousness. And in the *grand pas de deux* from *Aurora*, one remembers her regal entrance and the almost foolhardy abandon with which she plummets toward the floor in the closing measures of the duet.

Restless, Toumanova has moved from role to role, from company to company. She appeared as ballerina with the Ballet Russe de Monte Carlo, the Original Ballet Russe (headed by De Basil when Massine took over the first organization), Ballet Theatre, the Paris Opéra Ballet, the San Francisco Civic Ballet, and other organizations. Musical comedy and motion pictures (she married Casey Robinson, a Hollywood director) also borrowed her talents. Old ballets—*Giselle, Aurora, Swan Lake, Les Sylphides, Le Spectre de la Rose, Firebird*—interested her as much as (and sometimes more than) new works, new productions created especially for her.

Of the three baby ballerinas, Toumanova has earned for herself the most lasting success. With British companies in England, with French or international dance groups in France, in America, or in other quarters of the globe, she is always a very special star, a "black

132

pearl" indeed. One may smile at her stage hauteur and her movement melodramatics, but one may also savor and cherish those roles which she performs sensitively and that physical skill which sets ballet aflame.

Irina Baronova, Russian-born contemporary ballerina, one of the three famed "baby ballerinas" seen in America for the first time in 1933 when the Ballet Russe opened its first season here. Enjoyed a great success in Massine's first symphonic ballet, Les Présages. *She also created many principal parts in new works produced by the Ballet Russe and other companies. Baronova, married and a mother, is in retirement.*

Baronova, who also boasted a prodigious technique, was wholly different from Toumanova on stage. Blonde and small (both she and Toumanova have had to battle overweight from time to time), she brought to the stage a captivating innocence, a girlishness which Toumanova, even as a teen-ager, never seemed to possess. A batch of *pirouettes*—sometimes she did five or six in sequence, unsupported—appeared as a manifestation of youthful exuberance, and her infectious smile, her bounce, and her utterly feminine softness caused many a balletomane to murmur, "She's good enough to eat."

As a mere child, she first appeared in Paris in a Balanchine ballet, *Orphée aux Enfers,* and startled everyone with the aplomb with which she dashed off a complex series of turns, a sequence which, a generation before, would have scared a mature *prima ballerina* half to death. At the ripe age of thirteen, as a member of the Ballet Russe, she made a sensational success in Massine's first symphonic ballet, the controversial *Les Présages.*

133

IRINA BARONOVA
IN "COQ D'OR"

In the ensuing years, as a star of the Ballet Russe de Monte Carlo, the Original Ballet Russe, Ballet Theatre, and other companies, she created roles in *The Hundred Kisses*, *Choreartium*, *Le Beau Danube*, *Bluebeard*, *Helen of Troy*, and numerous other productions. But like Toumanova, Baronova was not divorced from the classics. She, too, danced in *Aurora's Wedding*, *Swan Lake*, *Le Spectre de la Rose*, and *Les Sylphides*. She delighted her public with gay roles in *Coppélia* and *La Fille Mal Gardée*, a difficult character part in *Petrouchka*, a shimmering Queen in *Coq d'Or*.

Firebird was also in Baronova's repertory, and an experience comparable to her landing on her head in *Les Sylphides* occurred during a performance in New York. These were the days of jealousies, of partisanships. No one dueled over his favorite any more but intrigues were rife. As the Firebird, Baronova flashed onto the stage and as she did so, her shoulder-straps broke, leaving her upper body bare. Her quick-thinking partner, Paul Petroff, placed his arm under hers and, holding the front of her costume in place, helped her finish her variation as modestly as possible. A later check of the garment showed that the straps had been cut to the breaking point by a razor. Who did it? No one knows, but someone did not want Baronova to dance.

Off-stage, Toumanova was always the ballerina. Baronova was not. True, she was lovely, gracious, and even glamorous, but she was a little girl, a young woman who had never had a real childhood and wanted to capture the fun she had missed. She loved to joke in a hearty, earthy way, and she liked to play games. Once, this renowned ballerina could have been discovered in a corner of a studio at Jacob's Pillow, the dance center in the Berkshire Hills, laughing and playing a rough game with her colleague, George

Skibine. For as others rehearsed and some artists awaited with dignity their call, Baronova and Skibine tried to see who could stamp on whose foot first.

Baronova, though childlike, was by no means childish. She learned English more quickly than any of her Russian compatriots and she could be found, games and jokes to the contrary, reading everything from the latest novels to books on American history and politics. Further, she was not greedy, as her artistic ancestor, Madeleine Guimard, appears to have been. On one occasion when an admirer took this baby ballerina to Cartier's in Paris and told her to pick anything her heart desired, she avoided diamonds and all items which seemed expensive—because it would have been in bad taste to select something too valuable just as it would have been in poor taste to refuse to accept a gift—and settled upon a toilet case with comb and brush. Her little selection, however, turned out to be made of purest, solid gold, and like the Ancient Mariner's albatross, in the months and years which followed it weighed upon her conscience as well as upon her muscles.

Like Toumanova, she essayed the fields of musical comedy and motion pictures, but, unlike the former, she has not found ballet irresistible. She returns to it from time to time, but her interest now, aside from wifely duties (she has been married twice) and motherhood, is acting. As a matter of fact, several of her friends have thought that Baronova went through a period when she actually did not like to dance. This was noticeable particularly around 1940, when the child prodigy was no more and the mature ballerina had yet to come. It was a transition period which made many unhappy, for although the fabulous technique was still there, a sense of tension prevailed and the infectious good spirits of the child gave way to a surprising stage soberness. Baronova, perhaps, was tired. She had studied ballet since babyhood and lived the demanding life of a star for many years. Maybe she wanted to play.

The transition was short, fortunately, and a ripening, glowing Baronova emerged to dance her way into everyone's heart. And if husband, children, and the drama steal her forever from the ballet stage, who will ever forget her buoyant, spinning solo in *La Fille Mal Gardée*; her lusty, comic, and voluptuous dancing of the triumphant wife in *Bluebeard*; the womanliness of her Swan Queen; the sweep of her long and lovely limbs in *Aurora*; her velocity mated with a smile?

Baronova and Toumanova were, speaking with respect to body mechanics, twirlers, and Tatiana Riabouchinska was a leaper. The third of the baby ballerinas lived in the air, and it was not contact with the earth—the grinding of a point through multiple turns or the sustaining of precarious balance upon the tip of a toe slipper in defiance of gravity's law—which gave excitement to her dancing. It was freedom to soar or, if she had to tread the ground, to float over it.

Tatiana Riabouchinska, one of the Russian-born "baby ballerinas," noted for her elevation, lightness, and speed, for her dancing of the "Prelude" in Les Sylphides, the title part in Coq d'Or, of the Florentine Maiden in Paganini, and in the "Bluebird" pas de deux from The Sleeping Beauty. Often appears as guest artist with various companies, and is closely associated with her husband, David Lichine, dancer and choreographer, in his enterprises.

The Swan Queen, Aurora, Giselle—these were not for Riabouchinska. To her belonged the fluttering Princess who emulates her captive Bluebird; the climbing, slashing, swooping, winged cockerel of *Coq d'Or;* the dreaming girl of *Le Spectre de la Rose;* the lovely child of *Le Beau Danube;* the enchanted Florentine maiden in *Paganini;* the airy, whispering "Prelude" in *Les Sylphides.* She was a good comedian, too, as she demonstrated so brilliantly in *Carnaval* (as Columbine) and as the lass with the flying pigtails in *Graduation Ball.* Where Toumanova provided the glitter and Baronova the glow to the trio of baby ballerinas, Riabouchinska touched it with an elusive, ethereal light.

It was natural that during the tumultuous renascence of ballet in the 1930's the stars should move from company to company in search of new audiences, new opportunities, better contracts. Baronova and Toumanova did just that, and so did Riabouchinska, who, following her debut with the Chauve-Souris in Paris, danced with an array of organizations including, of course, the Ballet Russe de Monte Carlo and Ballet Theatre, the Original Ballet Russe, the opera ballet in Buenos Aires, and the Ballets des Champs-Elysées.

Riabouchinska does not dance so frequently as she once did, preferring apparently to travel with her husband, the choreographer

TATIANA RIABOUCHINSKA

IN "COQ D'OR"

David Lichine, to wherever his assignments and commissions take him. Nor is she quite so light, quite so unearthly of motion as when she was a baby ballerina. But she must know that she has achieved the definitive characterizations in many ballets. Her "Prelude" in *Les Sylphides* has never been equaled, for here truly was a sylph moved by gentle breezes, silent, unearthly. And who could dance in *Paganini* as she danced? Her quick falls to the ground were as light as her soarings into space, and so quickly did she move that the eye could scarcely follow the bending, floating, dipping, spinning, running patterns of dance. As she danced, in this ballet, under the hypnotic spell of Paganini's near-diabolic music, so did she, through the magic of her performing, weave a spell around and about her audience. Nothing quite like it had been experienced in ballet before; Riabouchinska had brought new and late glory to the choreography of Michel Fokine.

Each of the baby ballerinas contributed something very special and personal to the art of ballet, but more important was their joint symbolizing of a new era in dance. Here, for the first time, were constantly traveling ballerinas brought up and trained amid hardships unknown to their immediate predecessors, who had developed and studied in the seclusion of a state school. They were mature before their time because life had hurried them along, because they needed jobs, because ballet was crying for something new.

Physically, they could outdance their seniors—although they had been taught by them (Preobrajenska, Kchessinskaya, and Egorova, to name but three)—and movements which had been regarded as the peculiar province of the virtuoso became almost commonplace. Thanks to them and their ability to perform the classics with in-

140

creased technical skills and whatever new actions a large group of modern choreographers devised, the range of ballet was extended. Without them, or their counterparts, many of Balanchine's demanding ideas would have come to naught or been delayed, and Massine could not possibly have brought his choreographic plans to full realization without their versatility. So if they attracted audiences because of their extreme youth and the novelty of their status (ballerinas at thirteen!), they also served the cause of dancing itself.

On the debit side, it can be said that they developed so fast technically that the nuances and the depths of performing and characterization were sometimes absent and never quite to be caught up with. Temporarily, they placed an unfair accent on the advantages of extreme youth, thus making it difficult for older ballerinas to convince an audience that with maturity comes deepening artistry. They also, because of their teen-age status, brought the traveling, hovering, fighting, protective "ballet mama" into the picture, and this figure, as any stage manager will record, has already done her bit toward increasing tension and tears backstage, as if there were not problems enough to begin with.

There are still further points of disapproval with respect to the arrival and influence of the baby ballerinas, but the advantages and contributions, choreographers and critics admit, far exceeded the wrongs. They were needed, as history has shown, to revitalize public interest in ballet, and they were needed by young and ambitious choreographers to bring a bigger, better, and fresher ballet to the stage. Although they were babies, they did a job for dance that no one else could do.

ALEXANDRA DANILOVA

Firebird

Le Beau Danube

PRIMA BALLERINA ASSOLUTA

Alexandra Danilova, contemporary ballerina, born and trained in Russia, came to America in 1933. Her annual tours of America with the Ballet Russe made her more familiar to Americans than almost any other ballerina. Her amazing versatility has brought her world renown. No longer with the Ballet Russe, Danilova has continued to perform, and a great deal of her time is devoted to teaching, partly in New York but mainly in Texas, where she has teaching headquarters at a school in Dallas.

What do you suppose are the reactions of Alexandra Danilova, trained in the Russian Imperial Ballet, when she sees the photograph of a pretty girl in a magazine or in an advertisement for a show and reads a caption which describes the girl in the picture as "Miss So-and-So, ballerina in . . ."? Is this pretty miss really a ballerina? Do toe shoes and *tutu* make the ballerina? Is a uniformed man a general or a woman with a racket necessarily a tennis champion? In America, there is no state ballet institution which regulates the training of the dancer, provides the successful student with a *corps de ballet* position, and promotes her from rank to rank as she earns her advancement. And so the girl who dances one leading role or, more often, just dances in a ballet company finds herself listed in feature stories or picture magazines as a ballerina. The ballet world, including the performers and discerning members of the public, knows that she is no such thing.

143

There is no doubt, however, that Alexandra Danilova is a ballerina, a *prima ballerina*. She had danced principal roles for almost a decade before the rank of ballerina was granted to her by the director of her company, and before that lay years of schooling and seasoning in ensemble assignments and small parts. Such unhurried and careful development has paid off, for Danilova has now been a ballerina for more than a quarter of a century, a star whose popularity has outlasted that of some of her juniors who, like hothouse plants, were pushed for early and quick blooming. Alexandra Danilova, on the other hand, is a hardy perennial.

Surprisingly, Danilova does not adhere to the tradition—although she does to the training—which made her a ballerina. Since there are no federal ballet companies, no real ballet academies (combining general education with dance training) in her adopted land, Danilova believes that dance rank is conferred by the public. When, for example, a pretty and talented girl is cast in the role of *Giselle* or in some other ballerina part, the audience, upon her entrance, says to itself, "Isn't she pretty?" or "Isn't she graceful?" or any of a number of pleasant comments. But when a true star, whether she is known by name or not to that particular public, makes her entrance (and perhaps she merely walks on), the public says "Ballerina." When Danilova walks onto the stage, there is no doubt. She is a ballerina, she is a "Queen of the Dance."

Many believe that Danilova would have been a great dancer no matter what her technical background had been. A friend, in an ecstatic moment, told her, "You would have been a dancer even if you had been born in a tribe in the Philippines." "What you mean?" said Danilova. Then there were explanations about the fact that, although she was a ballerina, she possessed instinctive dance qualities which would have made a dancer of her even if she had not had the formal training of the ballet. "Ah! like Isadora," she murmured, understanding.

As a child in Russia, Danilova had been deeply impressed by the dancing of Isadora Duncan, an artist so different from any in the ballet. Yet something of Isadora's freedom of movement, of her emotional force must have found a warm, unanalyzed response in the young student, for although Danilova was to become a classicist, an expert on traditional technique and period styles, she was never to be accused of sacrificing feeling for cold accuracy, of executing a movement instead of dancing it.

Danilova, as a matter of fact, was dancing long before she knew the word ballet. She was punished for vanity when she stood in front of a mirror and watched herself move and she was sent to ballet school when she was discovered standing on the tips of her toes. Ballet, at first, had nothing to do with it. Alexandra, little Choura, just liked to dance.

She liked to dance in spite of an early childhood filled with many changes and personal tragedy. Her father died when she was a tiny baby, and in quick succession her mother and grandmother passed away. Next, she was placed in the care of her godmother, only to be moved on shortly to the care of an affectionate and loving woman whom she came to call "Aunt." But this relationship was ended by death soon after she had entered the Imperial Theater School in St. Petersburg and the remainder of her upbringing was entrusted to a sort of stepsister (family relationships at this point were highly complicated), who became a loving guide and a helpful and devoted friend to the young student.

But Danilova's early life was, on the whole, a happy one. Her

family, both real and adopted, was not poor and the little girl enjoyed the best of care, holidays in the country, and the brand of
preliminary education which, in time, would lead to schooling at
an accepted institute and a society debut. Her aunt's decision to
apply for her niece's admission to the Imperial School changed all
those plans for the future. A mischievous child who had had her
relatives and governesses working overtime to keep an eye on her
was going to experience discipline, harsh discipline for the first time.

Choura, as she was called (and is still called by her friends),
was one of several hundred candidates applying for admission to
the school. About one half were eliminated by the medical exam-
iners and of the remainder only eighteen were chosen by the artistic
board. Choura was one of these.

As the years passed, her skills developed, and as a student she
had opportunities to perform children's parts with the ballet and to
appear in student performances. But the closing years of training
were not easy. World War I had brought its hardships and the
Revolution still more. The school (no longer "Imperial") and its
functions continued pretty much as before but food was scarce and
the hard-working youngsters found that they had to survive on
watery soup, potato skins, and very little bread. Survive they did,
and following graduation, one of their number, Alexandra Danilova,
joined the ranks of the professional dancers.

Like all dancers graduating from the state school, Danilova expected nothing more than *corps de ballet* assignments with the
state ballet. She was proud enough to be selected for front-row
work and marveled that at the end of her first season with the ballet
she was given the solo, "Prayer," in *Coppélia* to perform. Some
thirty years later, the ballerina who was to make the leading role

146

of the mischievous Swanhilda in the same ballet one of her matchless characterizations smiles as she recalls her solo debut and comments, "You can see what an innocent one I was in those days."

Toward the close of her second year with the Russian state ballet,
Danilova was cast in her first ballerina role (although she was not
yet to receive the rank of ballerina), the title part in *Firebird*. This
bit of casting almost caused a minor revolution in Russia—at least
in ballet circles—for Danilova was still a beginner. She danced it,
however, and with considerable success. There were also opportunities for dancing in experimental works for such choreographers
as the young George Balanchine, soon to become one of the world's
greatest choreographers.

Danilova, perhaps weary of memories of potato-skin diets and
the limitations of even a great ballet organization, determined to
leave Russia for study and performing elsewhere in Europe. With
governmental permission, she, Balanchine, and Tamara Geva joined
a small unit of Russian dancers and singers for a tour of Europe.
Although she did not realize it then, it was a farewell to her homeland and the beginning of a new career as a ballerina of international
renown.

The little group traveled through Western Europe, but engagements were not easy to come by. When it appeared that a return
to Russia was inevitable, fortune came to their aid and the dancers
were engaged by Serge Diaghilev as new members of his company,
then the greatest in the Western world. Here it was that Danilova
danced with some of the most famous stars of ballet, met the great
artists who surrounded Diaghilev, participated in modern ballets
so different from those she had known, helped the young Alicia
Markova in her development as an artist, became a ballerina.

Diaghilev's sudden death brought chaos to the ballet world. His company fell apart, scattered. Danilova danced in an operetta in London, but the moment a revival of a Russian ballet company for the West seemed possible, she was eager to return to the art which was her very life. Because times were hard and the launching of a new company difficult, she agreed to a nominal salary when she joined, as ballerina, the Russian Ballet directed by Colonel Wassily de Basil.

The love affair between Danilova and the American public commenced twenty-odd years ago when the De Basil Ballet arrived in this country.

The star was called upon to share honors with the "baby ballerinas," with Markova, with Mia Slavenska, and with others during her association with De Basil and later with Leonide Massine and his Ballet Russe de Monte Carlo. No matter what the publicity, however, Danilova remained the *prima ballerina* and the public knew it. And she became beloved because she was loyal. She danced in America year after year. She danced hard and she danced often. She danced as well for the public in a school auditorium in the Middle West as she did for a glittering audience at the Metropolitan.

In her tours, she did not rely on a favorite role or upon a style of dance. She danced in classical parts, modern ballets, symphonic ballets, comedies, melodramas, folk pieces, pantomimes. She danced when other ballerinas were ill or when they were new to her company and had not yet learned the repertory. Until recent seasons, she danced without rest, for audiences in American towns and cities demanded her presence on programs slated for them. When she walked onto a stage, people could say not only "Ballerina!" but also "Danilova!"

148

What vision, what memories does her name evoke? To some, it will be Danilova as the Queen of the Swans, imperious, womanly, enchanted. One can see the softness of her arms as she caresses her Prince or the stern power of an arm as she dismisses her swan maidens or the fluttering of those arms as the Queen-bird seeks to escape. And her feet! how they fly through the quick coda of her variation, fast but never blurred by fleetness.

Who can forget the grand waltz from *Gaité Parisienne* as the flirtatious glove seller dances with her baron? Here is sway and lilt and romance, but with no swooning, no droopy action. In the arms of her most nearly perfect partner, Frederic Franklin, Danilova dances the ecstasy of youth and, with Franklin, gives physical form to the sweep of a waltz. And then we can remember those legs— the most beautiful in all ballet—prancing through the cancan in *Boutique Fantasque*, strutting and kicking in *Le Beau Danube*, or floating like dream-magic in the sleepwalking scenes from *Night Shadow*.

There is the body which captures the accent of a phrase, rests uplifted on a musical echo, reflects lightness, strength, anguish, or joy. Even the eyelashes dance, in a face which can be piquant or regal or girlish, as Danilova brings a doll to life in *Coppélia*. Her entire body, her penetrating mind, and her enormous knowledge make possible this amazing range of dance expression. Whether she is the best Swan Queen, the best Giselle, the best cancan dancer is unimportant and even arguable, but what it true is that her Swan Queen, her Giselle, and her other characterizations are not copies. They are her own and different from those of any other ballerina.

She is a superb artist because she knows style as well as stylishness. A *pirouette*, a curtsy, a gesture will vary from role to role as

149

Swan Lake   Coppélia

Boutique Fantasque.

ALEXANDRA DANILOVA

Danilova analyzes the period in which a ballet is set and studies the behavior of a given character with respect to continent, country, region, background, customs, and century. And she is also an instinctive dancer, for she achieves dance effects that no one ever taught her and for which she has no explanation. As an example, one might point to her command of body dynamics, that aspect of movement which governs the ebb and flow of energy and which may be compared to the shading of colors in a painting or the loudness and softness achieved by the musician.

Once, when she read that she was in complete command of dynamics, she said, "What is zis deeneemeecs?" It was explained to her, but nothing more was said on the subject. A year later, when friends were criticizing adversely the performing of a visiting ballerina from Europe, Danilova remarked, "Ah, yes. Good style but no deeneemeecs. She always soapsuds, never cake of soap." What better definition of movement dynamics could one want, and from an artist whose training program never used the word or explained the principle?

Danilova, although she represents the tradition of the Russian Imperial Ballet and is, perhaps, the last of its home-trained ballerinas still performing outside Russia, is curious and open to new ideas. She could not understand *modern dance* in America, but she blamed no one but herself. "I study it," she promised, and she did. On another occasion, she heard that America's great ethnic dancer, La Meri, was going to present a Hindu dance version of *Swan Lake*. "I do not want to see it. A swan sliding its neck sideways [and this she demonstrated] over shoulders? No!" Then, a fresh young upstart muttered, "But Madame, have you ever seen a swan in *arabesque*?" The answer: "You are right. I go." She went, and two

151

distantly related Swan Queens became fast friends.

After twenty years of one-night stands, Alexandra Danilova has left the Ballet Russe de Monte Carlo for teaching and "a slow retirement" from the stage. A few more performing seasons are left to her as guest star with various companies and as a soloist with symphony orchestras. No one wants her to retire, although everyone recognizes that she must do so one day. Danilova knows this best of all but she does not want a series of sniffling farewells. She came to America with gaiety in her heart and in her unequaled legs, and she will quit the stage gaily, disappearing slowly from the eyes of the public.

As long as she lives, however, Danilova will never desert the ballet. As a teacher of dancing, she will unquestionably bring to American boys and girls knowledge of a ballet tradition old and honored, knowledge of a vast repertory of dance, knowledge of "deeneemeecs." The "baby ballerinas" may have been better copy; Markova, the greatest *Giselle* of our day, may have won fame and a top salary through the ethereal beauty of her dancing; Nana Gollner may have been able to turn faster and reach higher with a leg; Zorina may have been more beautiful; others, such as Milada Mladova, may have been more photogenic (she replaced Danilova in a motion picture version of *Gaité Parisenne*), but Danilova was America's *prima ballerina*.

Some years ago, the curtain rose on the closing ballet of an opening-night program at the Metropolitan Opera House. The company was the Ballet Russe de Monte Carlo; the ballet, *Gaité Parisienne*. As Danilova made her entrance as the glove seller, the house cheered. She had been seen in the part for many, many years; a world première had preceded this ballet and other important dance offerings had been on the bill; but this was it, this was ballet and here was the ballerina. The ovation stopped the show, drowned out the music as the ballerina, for the first time in her life, stopped dancing midway in an opening phrase to acknowledge the tribute of her followers.

An ovation for Danilova in *Gaité* became a habit on opening night of each subsequent season in New York, and when the farewell with the Ballet Russe de Monte Carlo came, it was, of course, *Gaité* which brought the long association to an end. There were flowers at this leave-taking in Texas, flowers from stagehands and wardrobe personnel and dancers as well as from the public, and a ballerina wept. But this, nevertheless, was, in a sense, a happy occasion, for it provided final proof that Danilova was more than a *prima ballerina*. In the Russia of Imperial days, the chosen one of the Imperial court was named the *prima ballerina assoluta*. Russia had only one in its whole history. America had no court, no all-powerful being to bestow such a title. The American public, without knowing the term and its meaning, had, through its recognition of and love for her, crowned Alexandra Danilova, now a citizen of the United States, with the most coveted of honors, the reverence and affection due a *prima ballerina assoluta*.

"LITTLE ALICIA, MINIATURE PAVLOVA"

Alicia Markova, contemporary English ballerina, created many and diversified roles for the Vic-Wells (now Sadler's Wells) Ballet, and has also appeared with Anton Dolin in companies under their own direction, with the Ballet Russe, with Ballet Theatre, and with other groups. Her most famous enactment is that of Giselle and she is considered by most as the finest modern exponent of that classical role.

The choreographer of *Giselle?* Who bothers to notice? The ballerina? Ah! now we are getting somewhere. Perhaps it is Danilova or Toumanova, Alonso or Fonteyn or Gollner. Perhaps it is even the incomparable Markova. This is what matters, for does not *Giselle* belong to the ballerina? Is not this *"Hamlet* of the dance" her test, her trial by fire, just as *Hamlet* itself proffers power or panic to a Barrymore, a Gielgud, an Evans, an Olivier?

No one, however, forgets that Shakespeare wrote *Hamlet,* whereas few of today's public consider that without Coralli and Perrot the patterns of *Giselle* might never have come to the theater of dance to be seen and cherished for more than one hundred years. One must not, then, overlook the contributing geniuses of Coralli and Perrot (the choreographers); Gautier, Saint-Georges, and Coralli (the authors); Adam (the composer); and those later choreographers and ballet masters responsible for necessary restagings of an antique masterpiece. Conversely, it must be stressed that all these talents would have been in vain without the presence of the ballerina. Carlotta Grisi made of *Giselle* an enduring classic.

Alicia Markova, more than any other ballerina, renewed *Giselle's* immortality for the twentieth century.

Like Giselle, little Alicia was frail, frail in the body but by no means frail in heart or head. Because she was knock-kneed and fragile, Lilian Alicia Marks was ordered by the family doctor to take up some kind of dancing, and so at nine years of age the little girl who was to become the first internationally famous ballerina to be produced by England enrolled in Miss Thorne's Dancing Academy.

A year later, in 1920, when she was ten, Alicia made her professional debut in a Christmas pantomime, and by that time it was clear to the girl's mother that dancing was to have more than therapeutic value for her daughter. The next step was to assure the very best of training for "the miniature Pavlova," and study in deadly earnest commenced under Princess Serafina Astafieva, a graduate of the Russian Imperial School, a former member of the Diaghilev Ballet, and the first Russian dancer to open a school in Alicia's home town, London.

Under Astafieva's tutelage, the big talent in the frail body began to blossom. In recitals, the child actually was advertised as "the miniature Pavlova," and in many ways she resembled—at that time and later—her idol. For the child Pavlova had also been delicate and ailing, and the adult ballerina possessed those qualities of lightness, effortlessness, floating romanticism which were to be reproduced in the mature Markova.

Three years with Astafieva transformed a student into a dancer, for during a visit to the studio, Diaghilev saw her and engaged her at the tender age of fourteen for his company. Other transformations took place. Astafieva had schooled her in the style and tech-

155

ACT

GISELLE

Act I

ALICIA MARKOVA

nique of Russian ballet. Diaghilev, upon her joining the company in 1924, changed Lilian Alicia Marks into Alicia Markova. Her hair-style was also altered to conform with the severe lines of the Russian classic dancer, and the new influences were completed through the friendship and guidance of a Diaghilev star, Alexandra Danilova.

Little Miss Marks disappeared. "With Diaghilev you had to forget your nationality," Markova recalls. "He would not even permit me to take the tests prepared by the Royal Academy of Dancing. 'No!' he said. 'You'd probably try to wear your medals in *Giselle*.' So it was not until after his death that I became associated with the Royal Academy and with the development of ballet in England. But my name? I would have changed it anyhow. For the theater one needs fantasy. . . ."

During her years with the Diaghilev Ballet—until the great impresario's death in 1929—Markova advanced from modest assignments through solo parts to the creation of a leading role in *Le Rossignol* by Balanchine. There were also stellar duties for her in such works as *La Chatte* and *Cimarosiana*, and at the time of his death, Diaghilev was planning a revival of *Giselle* in which Markova would have shared the title role with Olga Spessivtzeva.

It was a rich period for the young dancer. She held a position of some importance in the finest ballet company outside of Russia, she was receiving training from the great maestro Enrico Cecchetti, and she was being molded into a star with a very special style. Diaghilev must surely have recognized her inherent lyricism, her incipient skill in evoking the elusive flavors of lyric fantasy, for he continually scolded her for her virtuoso tendencies. It is difficult for us today to fancy a Markova throwing herself into multiple spins or leaping with abandon or otherwise indulging in physical violence. Yet she reminds us that she once did spin fast and kick high and that Diaghilev snorted, "Go to the circus where you belong." And thus a precise, gentle, easy, ethereal Markova was patterned.

With the passing of Diaghilev, ballet in Western Europe shuddered and nearly perished. Opera ballet could not possibly replace the glittering organization he had created, and it was left to his dispersed heirs—choreographers, dancers, *régisseurs*—of various nationalities to shift for themselves as individuals or to try to unite a reorganized company along Diaghilev lines.

For a season, Markova shifted for herself. She appeared as a dancer in a London stage presentation and commenced her associations with Marie Rambert's Ballet Club and the new Camargo Society. With these two groups and, shortly thereafter, with the Vic-Wells Ballet (later to become the Sadler's Wells Ballet), Markova participated in those stirring plans and experiments which were to lead English ballet to new heights of honor and achievement in the world of dance.

She created roles, totally different from those she had known in her Diaghilev days, in ballets choreographed by Ninette de Valois (now the director of the Sadler's Wells Ballet) and by the young Frederick Ashton, destined to grow into England's most celebrated choreographer. She danced in the rollicking *Façade*, the mysterious *The Haunted Ballroom*, the gay *Les Rendezvous*. In *The Rake's Progress*, her ability as a mime was tested, and other creations called for her to be gay or sad, fleet or slow, *sur les pointes* or in tap shoes, remote or real. These were fine days for Markova. Her versatility was tested, her talent challenged, her youth wisely exploited

159

by an equally youthful ballet enterprise. But still finer days were to come.

During her second year with the Vic-Wells Ballet, full-length versions of *Swan Lake*, *Nutcracker*, and *Giselle* were mounted especially for her. None of these ballets is (or was) her exclusive property, yet her international reputation rests almost solidly upon them or extracts from them along with another all-time favorite, *Les Sylphides*. Other ballerinas dance these roles (and superbly), and Markova herself has danced in any number of different ballets with enormous success. Nevertheless, she is somehow identified with these classics, perhaps because they evoke a gracious past and a world of fairies, just as the dancing Markova seems to be a vision from the Romantic age of ballet, a figure as light as the sylph or fairy or wili or swan she portrays.

It was impossible, however, for Markova to belong to England alone. Diaghilev, without affecting her personal "Englishness" or tampering with her loyalty to her homeland and its art progress, had started her on a pathway which was to lead to international prestige. The expanding of her interests commenced in 1935 with the founding of the Markova-Dolin Ballet, the first English ballet organization to perform throughout Great Britain. With Anton Dolin, star dancer, choreographer, brilliant restager of the classics, and astute director, she formed a partnership. This artistic union, for years to come, survived changes in company, in projects, and in geographical headquarters.

By 1938, Markova had completed her first period of service to dance in England. She had given unstintingly of her talents and energies to the Vic-Wells, she had appeared with the Ballet Rambert and the Camargo Society. At last free of Diaghilev's orders, she was able to join the activities of the Royal Academy of Dancing and to help in the staging of a *Les Sylphides* under that organization's auspices. Together with Dolin and their group, she brought the growing beauties of British ballet dancing to the provinces of her nation. But the time had come to move on.

That year—1938—saw the union of Markova with the Ballet Russe de Monte Carlo for appearances in Europe and the Americas. New audiences marveled at her dancing of the classics, but they also cheered her performances in new roles. Among these additions to her repertory were principal parts in *Rouge et Noir*, Leonide Massine's dance visualization of Shostakovich's First Symphony, and the same choreographer's *Vienna—1814*. The first, which stressed wave-like movements of the spine (something of an innovation in ballet at the time), provided Markova with a part which was not concerned with academic movements and which called for a subtle evocation of mood rather than specific characterization. Massine, as Ashton had done earlier, created roles for Markova which, at first glance, seemed remote from the ballerina's special idiom, yet both were successful in their experiments and Markova noted that "Ashton and Massine could see things in me that had never been exploited before." This attitude delighted Markova, for in spite of her pre-eminence in traditional ballets of a romantic nature she says today that "the ballerina should not be expert in just one style but ready for anything the choreographer demands."

With Ballet Theatre, which she joined in 1941, Markova had opportunities not only to present her celebrated enactments of *Giselle*, *Swan Lake* (one act), and other classical ballets, but also to appear in new roles. Once again, Massine provided her with a new type of assignment in the gypsy *Aleko*, Antony Tudor cast

161

her as the immortal heroine of his dance treatment of *Romeo and Juliet*, and Dolin, in his restaging of the Victorian *Pas de Quatre*, proved incontrovertibly that Alicia Markova was truly the twentieth-century heiress of Taglioni. Here, in the *Pas de Quatre* and in the magic of Markova's dancing, one seemed to see the improbable poses of old lithographs reborn upon a contemporary stage. She poised upon a tiny *pointe* as if the floor were as delicate as a flower, her leaps appeared to be propelled by zephyrs, her fragile arms—slightly contracted to indicate Taglioni's concern over the length of such arms—rested on air.

Three years with Ballet Theatre were enough, and Markova, with Dolin, moved on to Broadway, to the theater of musical comedy (*Seven Lively Arts*) as the highest-paid ballerina in the world and one eager to bring classical dancing to the popular theater. With the end of World War II, travel was once again possible for this quiet yet restless star. The Markova-Dolin Company was re-formed for an American tour, and guest appearances with Ballet Theatre (in *Firebird*), a season with the Original Ballet Russe (directed by Colonel de Basil), and tours of Central America, the Orient, and South Africa as the Markova-Dolin unit followed in quick succession. A brief season in 1949 with the Ballet Russe de Monte Carlo was capped by a return to England—home, remembrance, renewal—and the founding of a new dance company (with Dolin), the Festival Ballet.

By 1952, Markova had again taken wing. She severed connections with Dolin and the Festival Ballet and set out upon an independent career as a soloist available as guest star with major ballet companies and opera ballet, as a concert dancer (assisted by a male partner), and as a television personality.

One could hardly keep track of her transcontinental, transoceanic travels, of her shifting theatrical commitments. But one could follow her creed of duty, her belief that all performers owe a tremendous obligation to the public. "Sickness or death of a near one," she says, "are unimportant. What you come out with on stage is all that matters." It is this very sense of obligation, rather than vanity or snobbery, which causes her to insist upon a star dressing room. "So much depends upon the star being free, clear, concentrated" that backstage turmoil must be avoided, and since the star must guide a performance on stage, it follows that she requires suitable quarters for preparation off stage.

Markova is, of course, a trouper, and she will, when necessary, share dressing rooms, cubicles, or screen arrangements. But she is a star and she expects to be treated as one. Furthermore, she has little patience with those who advocate starlessness in theatrical enterprises. No stars? Ridiculous! "The audience will make the star." And what is a star? What is a ballerina? Markova replies, "She is half-character, half-self."

In *Giselle* and other classics, for example, Markova engages in exhaustive research. She studies the period of a ballet, she studies the musical score, she finds out all she can about a balletic character and its interpretations by predecessors; but once the details of research are assimilated, the personal element is released to complete the definition of a new role. As Giselle, Markova, then, gives us a stage character, but she also gives us something of Markova. The same process is pursued during her creation of a contemporary role. As Juliet, she read the play anew, studied the words for phrasing and meaning and drama, and then, through

163

Tudor's choreography, sought to translate meaningful words into meaningful action.

Little, knock-kneed Lilian Marks has changed. Her teachers— Astafieva, Cecchetti, Legat, Egorova, Celli—gave her technical disciplines; Diaghilev and the Russian ballet transformed her from an English girl into a continental; world tours and the successful interpretation of some of ballet's greatest roles made her an international star. "At first," she recalls, "I was a technician and less of an interpreter, but by the time I joined Ballet Theatre I was commencing to graft characterization onto dance technique."

For a brief period (in the mid-1940's), characterization tended to exert too strong an influence upon her technique, for her interest in roles such as that of the fragile Giselle led her to "under-move." She avoided, probably unconsciously, anything resembling high leg extensions or multiple turns or anything hinting at energy. A return to London in 1948, however, brought an end to this attitude and Markova hastened to compose those differences existing between fragility and agility. But fragility, daintiness, romantic elusiveness still interest her more than other dance possibilities. She may, as she says, like variety, and she is certainly equipped to accomplish anything a choreographer may demand of her. *Giselle*, however, remains her favorite ballet and the one through which—as she believes herself—she has contributed most to the art of dancing.

And anyone who has beheld Markova's Giselle cannot fail to recognize her dance genius, for here is myth and fancy reborn in terms of movement as Markova gently but inexorably carries her heroine from joyous innocence and sweet love through madness and self-destruction to an undying solicitude which spans the abyss between a restless death and mortal love. She is ever delicate, ever unreal, ever a creature of that fantasy which she believes essential to the theater. Effortlessness characterizes everything she does, yet her sister ballerina and great, good friend Alexandra Danilova once served breakfast in bed to Markova and explained her actions to a surprised group of week-end guests with a terse, "Alicia works so hard."

NORA KAYE IN
"PILLAR OF FIRE"

Thirteen

"THE DUSE OF THE DANCE"

Nora Kaye, New York-born ballerina, became a star overnight in 1942 when she danced the principal role in Antony Tudor's ballet, Pillar of Fire, produced by Ballet Theatre at the Metropolitan Opera House. She is considered the greatest dramatic ballerina of the day, for not only has she brought the qualities of an actress to modern roles in ballets by Tudor, Jerome Robbins, and Agnes de Mille, but she has also invested many traditional parts with fresh dramatic meanings.

Usually the road is long and the way is hard, for stardom does not come easily. Occasionally, however, a star is born overnight. Or so it seems. The labor, the dedication, the anguish which precede such an event are forgotten in the glittering immediacy of a theatrical birth. And the artist, in advance, can never be sure that this is the moment. Perhaps, when the curtain falls, she will still be a soloist, even a principal, but not yet a star, not yet a ballerina, and she will have to wait for another time and another opportunity.

Nora Kaye did not have to wait. When the curtain fell on the first performance of *Pillar of Fire*, April 8, 1942, a star had been born. More than twenty curtain calls were demanded by an audience which made the Metropolitan Opera House echo with applause and cheers. An actress, weeping with excitement, murmured, "God! I would have given my whole career to have had this role." And alone on the great stage was a girl hardly more than twenty, yesterday a valued and dependable member of Ballet Theatre, tonight a ballerina.

The applause was not for Kaye alone. It was for Antony Tudor, who had created a masterpiece; for Hugh Laing, who had added another great characterization to his list of achievements; for a company which had danced flawlessly. But for Tudor, Laing, and the company, it was an extension (and a monumental one) of fame already earned and recognized. For Nora Kaye, it was the bestowal of fame.

Here was a new kind of ballerina. The test had not come with *Swan Lake* or *Giselle*, but in a new ballet which owed as much to the principles of *modern dance* as it did to the traditional vocabulary of theatrical dancing. There were *pirouettes*, there were *grands jetés*, and there were *arabesques*, but what made *Pillar of Fire* and

168

what made Nora Kaye a star was not merely physical movement but, rather, meaningful movement.

From the very start, it was clear to all that here was a dance actress. There was no *grande entrée*, no *tutu*, no escorting cavalier. She sat with respectable erectness upon the steps of a respectable house. A hand brushed the cheek, the head twisted as if a modest Victorian neckline were too confining. Here was propriety, frustration, but a gesture, a slight motion indicated the presence of passion beneath a stern exterior.

The plot of *Pillar of Fire* was not really new, not particularly fresh, not even very profound, but its treatment was all of these things. Hagar, straight and proper, was in love. The man appeared to prefer her younger and gayer sister, and Hagar, looking at her prim and settled older sister, seemed to see in her a mirror of herself to be, empty and spinsterish. And so Hagar, in desperate defiance, gave her body to a libertine who lived and reveled in a twisted, evil house across the way from her own impeccable dwelling. Remorse, reaffirmation, and rediscovery followed as Hagar found tenderness and love in the man she had sought and thought she had lost.

Tudor's choreographic realization of this basic and simple plot was a miracle of emotional penetration and of character definition. Like *modern dance's* great star, Martha Graham, he was concerned with revealing the inner man and not merely telling a surface story. In Hagar's initial gestures, we witnessed the overt manifestations of a restless spirit; in the *grand jeté* which propelled her into the arms of the libertine, the defiant drive of the desperate was disclosed; hands pulling a skirt tight around a crouching body indicated the wearer of a cloak of shame and a frenetic turn in *arabesque* told of the wild rush for an escape to other planes, to cleaner air.

169

And not only did Hagar reveal her passions through gesture (danced gesture) and the big movements of dance itself, but her temptations, her doubts, and her indecisions were symbolized by two groups, the Lovers-in-Innocence and the Lovers-in-Experience, which, like a mute Greek chorus, echoed and omened those conflicts of desire which beset the heroine.

Here, in *Pillar of Fire*, was a ballet which represented a faultless and facile and profound fusing of contemporary and traditional dance elements, and here, in Nora Kaye, was a new type of ballerina, a dancer destined to be called "the Duse of the dance." That dramatic skill, which was to lead to a flattering comparison with the great and almost legendary Italian actress, Eleanora Duse, was partly inherent and partly acquired, for Kaye was not first an actress. She was a dancer.

This native New Yorker commenced dance lessons and even performing when she was but a child. Training at the Metropolitan Opera Ballet School led to appearances at the Metropolitan in children's ballets, and by the time she was fifteen, Nora Kaye, a youthful veteran, was ready to dance with the American Ballet when it became the official company at the Opera. Next came a stint with the *corps de ballet* at the Radio City Music Hall, engagements as a dancer in a series of musical comedies, and, finally, association in 1939 with the new Ballet Theatre as *corps de ballet* girl and minor soloist.

Studies with Michel Fokine (her idol), Vilzak, Shollar, and Antony Tudor, who was to make her a star, enabled her to extend her basic talent, to broaden her knowledge of style, to stir her intellect into exploring for herself the potentialities, the endless potentialities of that art she was eager to serve.

170

Which of her dance masters did the most for her? It would be impossible to say. But surely Antony Tudor prepared her for the part of Hagar as no ballerina had ever been prepared before for a given role. Technical direction was but a small part of the process, for Tudor made his key dancers, and especially Kaye, live with the ballet during the period—almost two years—of its creation. Hagar was discussed not only as a theatrical role but as a human being. Her whole life was imagined; her childhood, her friends, her region, her era (although they would never come to the stage) were talked about in detail. When the time came to dance Hagar, the dancer knew her, knew why she was in the emotional turmoil she was in, knew what frustrations and compulsions had led her to that point of drama which saw the start of the ballet itself.

Here, then, was that intensive training which was to carry Nora Kaye to triumph in *Pillar of Fire* and to focus her attentions upon the dramatic element in all roles from *Swan Lake* and *Giselle* to *Facsimile* and *The Cage*. This dramatic approach to classical assignments has led to unorthodoxies, to adverse criticism, and to passing mistakes. But it has brought new life to many a ballet. In *Swan Lake*, for example, Nora Kaye has dared to question the choreography. There is, however, no haughtiness in this, no attempt to downgrade the choreographer, but merely an effort to find out what he meant by a given movement and not to take as gospel some other ballerina's instructions concerning the choreographer's intentions.

Kaye was worried by that passage in the one-act version of *Swan Lake* in which the Queen of the Swans, startled by the sudden arrival of the Prince, seeks to escape. She pushes away from him (balletically, of course!), turns aside, floats on an *arabesque*, runs,

171

flutters. But in the midst of this she is called upon to strike an *attitude* supported by the Prince. How come? Is she or is she not still seeking to escape? Kaye wondered. She could not and would not change Petipa, so she tried to discover what the choreographer had intended and she decided that the *attitude*, if it were accented properly, would seem like a pulling away from the Prince rather than merely a vertical balance. This she did and the whole scene took on fresh power and new logic.

Occasionally, her experiments may displease. Again in *Swan Lake*, she heavily accented the bending of the body and the forward thrust of the arms in the *adagio*, but she was taken to task by the distinguished ballet expert and editor of *Dance News*, Anatole Chujoy. "Okay, Choujoie" (as she calls him in mercilessly wrenched French), "I guess you're right, but it was so bird-like!"

As Giselle, she has also been a nonconformist. "I don't believe in playing Giselle like a ballerina out slumming," she avers. To her, Giselle is a peasant and should be performed as such. She has respect for, but little interest in, that kind of characterization which suggests that Giselle is a glittering ballerina thinly disguised for the sake of the plot. So in *Giselle* Kaye is the peasant whose dancing and miming combine the gaucheries of a village lass with the unescapable smoothness of a dance tradition. One sees, of course, ballet and ballerina, but Kaye endeavors to give us a simple maid, gay in her meeting with romance, heart-rendingly tragic in her discovery of her lover's true identity, half-real and half-fantastic in her guise of a restless ghost-maiden whose love spans the barrier between the dead and the living.

That Nora Kaye was going to be unlike all other ballerinas was clearly demonstrated on the day following her spectacular success in *Pillar of Fire*. She was asked what the difference was between an American ballerina (a rare creature) and a Russian ballerina (ruler of the ballet since Diaghilev had brought Russian ballet to the world). In a joking reference to the type of tale which the Russian artist tended to relate, Miss Kaye announced, and in her rousing New York accent, "All I can say is that I wasn't born in a boxcar while escaping the Russian Ravelooshun." With that comment, with her performance in *Pillar of Fire*, with her desire for experimentation, Nora Kaye founded a new class of ballerinas.

She became the despair of press agents and worried friends who wished to glamorize the new star off stage as well as on. But Kaye was incorrigible, for her wit and her good sense kept her from pretending that she was something she was not. She had not been born in a fleeing boxcar and she was not a product of the Imperial Theater. She was a New Yorker nurtured in show business. To the stage she brought glamor and fierce dramatic power, and to interviews she brought not only her humor but a deep knowledge of dance and its artistic forces. But away from the theater she preferred (and still does) to be herself, recognized as Nora Kaye, the star, but permitted to behave like Nora Kaye, the New Yorker.

Once, when she visited the Rainbow Room with friends, a trip to the roof after dinner seemed like a delightful idea. Everyone looked through the telescope at the stars and almost everyone discovered handsome views of Jupiter, Mars, or Venus. Not Nora Kaye. No stargazing for her. She looked through the telescope and shouted, "Whaddya know! There's my laundry on Sixty-sixth Street!"

Her irrepressible comments (when serious, both diction and vocabulary are those of a profound artist) even invade the theater and occasionally share honors with her most demanding roles, al-

173

though the audience is unaware of this. Once, in *Pillar of Fire*, one of the dancers suffered an acute muscle cramp on stage and finally succeeded in reaching the wings, where three of Ballet Theatre's young male dancers assembled with first aid suggestions and sympathies. Unfortunately, the three should have been on at that moment to assist Hagar in a complex lift. One of the trio dashed onto the stage just as Miss Kaye, improvising brilliantly, leapt by murmuring, "Where the hell is everybody?"

It follows that Nora Kaye, dramatic dancer, is also an accomplished comedian in the theater as well as in real life. As the Russian ballerina in Antony Tudor's fine satire of a Russian-Italian-French ballerina tangle, *Gala Performance*, she caricatures unmercifully her boxcar sisters. She plays the part broadly, leering at the audience, milking curtain calls, crowning displays of virtuosity with an expression which seems to say "How about that!" Only once was Miss Kaye frustrated in her delineation of this part. A real, live Russian ballerina had just finished dancing a particularly flashy *pas de deux* and she had danced it to the hilt. Before the curtain went up on *Gala*, a despondent Kaye said to the director, "Well, she's already done the part, and short of taking my teeth out and tossing them over the footlights, I can't think of any way to make this look like a comedy."

Her reputation, naturally, is not based upon *Pillar* and *Gala*. Not only has she achieved success in *Swan Lake* and *Giselle* (both in the title part and as the best Queen of the Wilis except for Danilova), but she has made the role of the unhappy bride in Tudor's *Lilac Garden* exclusively her own, she has triumphed in the same choreographer's *Romeo and Juliet*, and she has given remarkable performances in such diverse works as *Facsimile, On Stage!, The*

Gift of the Magi, The Age of Anxiety, Fall River Legend, Mother Goose Suite, and *The Cage.*

There are many who recognize her supreme position as a dramatic dancer but who do not admit her excellence as a classical ballerina. And they have a point, for she is not at her best in ballets without plot, nor in works of gentle mood which stress line and lyricism. Her Princess Aurora, though regal, is harsh, and the very movements which become her as the commanding, remorseless Queen of the Wilis do not fit her quite so well as the sweet and gentle Aurora. Yet her dancing of the difficult ballerina part in the "Black Swan" *pas de deux* is exciting indeed, for she makes virtuosity serve characterization as she defines a teasing, arrogant, glittering woman. As a matter of fact, the slenderest excuse for drawing character or projecting the varied hues of human emotions is sufficient for Kaye to explore the possibilities of a role and to give her audiences memories of an unforgettable adventure.

After a decade as dancer, soloist, and finally ballerina of Ballet Theatre, she suddenly left the company which had seen her jump to stardom and the repertory upon which her fame, both in America and Europe, rested. As a new ballerina with the New York City Ballet, she could not, at first, hope to match the fabulous Maria Tallchief, whose many roles had been faultlessly tailored to her remarkable talents by Balanchine. Furthermore, her style was different from those of the other artists in the Balanchine-dominated company, and the repertory had little or nothing to offer her. She struggled with a Balanchine *Pas de Trois* and another straight classical part in yet another Balanchine work and made a pleasant impression in a delicately haunting scene in the same choreographer's *Bourrée Fantasque.* But in none of these was she or is she particu-

larly impressive. Her position in the world of ballet was saved by
one who had choreographed for her before, by a colleague who had
also won stardom and choreographic fame with Ballet Theatre. He
was, of course, Jerome Robbins, and the ballet he created for her
was *The Cage*.

Once again an audience roared, for *The Cage*, controversies not-
withstanding, was a hit. Robbins, now associate artistic director of
the New York City Ballet, had created for Kaye a savage ritual
dealing with a female sect, half-insect and half-human, dedicated to
the destruction of the male. As the novice trained in the art of
obliterating the male, tempted by romance, and finally reaffirmed in
the ways of her horrid sect, Nora Kaye gave a monumental performance which fascinated as it terrified. Here was great dancing—not
just ballet dancing or just modern dancing, but a way of dance
which revealed all of an artist's expressional powers. Here was one
who was, unmistakably, the great dramatic ballerina of our time.

And whether we are watching the tortured actions of a Hagar in
Pillar of Fire, the smothered desires of a Caroline in *Lilac Garden*,
the remembered dreams of a maiden in *Mother Goose*, the hysteria
of an insecure woman in *Facsimile*, the feral stance of the amazon
in *The Cage*, the desperate fear of Lizzie Borden in Agnes de Mille's
Fall River Legend, the sweet caresses of a Juliet, the embattled
fouetté of a Russian ballerina in *Gala Performance*, or the tragic
descent of a star in Tudor's *La Gloire*, we may be sure that we are
watching one who is truly "the Duse of the dance."

A CUBAN STAR AND HER COLLEAGUES

Alicia Alonso, Cuban ballerina, head of her own company and school in Havana and prima ballerina of Ballet Theatre. She has been hailed in modern as well as in classical ballets, but she is best known for her Giselle. She has won a large following in Europe as well as in the Americas for her skill, both physical and dramatic, in tragedies, comedies, fantasies, and non-narrative, pure dance ballets. The title of "Dama" has been granted her by the government of her native land.

A bandaged ballerina. What could be more pitiful, more tragic, than immobility for one whose life is dedicated to the consummate beauty of motion? Yet Alicia Alonso, one of the world's great dance stars, lay for a year in bed, her eyes bandaged, her emotions held in check so that she could neither laugh nor cry. Her hard muscles became soft and the powerful techniques she had built up over the years slipped silently away.

But Alonso, though immobile, was not inactive. With her bandaged eyes she seemed to see herself on the stage. She recognized faults in those performances which she had danced for musical comedy, the American Ballet Caravan, and Ballet Theatre audiences and, in her mind, she commenced to correct them. In the evenings, she danced for her dancer-producer husband, Fernando, but only with her hands, as the aging Guimard had done in recreating with fleet fingers her past triumphs. And Fernando criticized as the digital substitutes for legs danced across the counterpane.

ALICIA ALONSO IN
"AURORA'S WEDDING"

There was time also in which to dream, and the dream was almost always of Giselle, of ways to portray her, to reveal the drama of which she was a part, to dance her incredibly difficult measures. At long last, the bandages were removed. The operation had been a success and blindness had been averted. But could the once fragile eyes stand the strains of performing, the blinding lights, the sudden movements, the pounding blood? No one was certain and permission to start dancing was postponed. Alonso, however, did not wait. From her Havana home, she sneaked to class and she practiced hard. No ill effects. Then a bad accident to her head. Still no ill effects. The eyes were cured. A cable was dispatched to Lucia Chase, co-director of Ballet Theatre: "I'm ready to come back."

It was more than a comeback; it was a new career, for the promising soloist, who had risen from the ranks of the *corps de ballet*, was now ready to become a ballerina. She did not have to wait long for her opportunity. Markova fell ill. Could Alonso dance *Giselle*? "Certainly," although she had performed it only with her fingers. Success was immediate and the Cuban ballerina was hailed as the heiress apparent to Markova.

She was still, however, only an heiress and not the wearer of the crown, and that rankled, but she deserved no more than this title, for she tended to imitate the matchless British ballerina. She had not yet drawn, fully and independently, her own Giselle. With each performance of the role she improved, and one day she presented the public with a Giselle which many considered to be the equal of Markova's.

In the first act, a Latin passion suffused her characterization. Her flirtatious dancing with Albrecht and her own stunning variation were performed with a peasant lustiness quite different from that tremulous fragility which Markova brought to the role. The mad scene, too, was rich in passion, almost angry, yet utterly poignant in its wildness. But there was lyricism, also, in the softly spiraling arms which seemed to say, "Let us be joyous in dance," and suspenseful floating was to be found in the arcs described in space by slowly moving legs.

The lightness, the mercurial softness essential to the second act were also realized as Giselle, a ghost-maiden, reached across the boundary separating life from death to touch the living with a last tenderness, to protect a lover from an evil, nighttime magic. In runs, in lifts, in *adagio* passages, Alonso was like mist, materializing into human form in the arms of her distraught Albrecht and fading away into the dusk. Her space-traveling *entrechats* were like fireflies flickering in the twilight, and her fleet turns, darting leaps, and beckoning arms were those of a Wili, commanded to lure the living into a dance of death.

Great as she is in this immortal classic, it is not hers exclusively. Sometimes she surpasses Markova (since almost all performers have their ups and downs), sometimes not, for at her best, Markova is unsurpassable. And other ballerinas—Danilova, Ulanova, Fonteyn, Slavenska, Gollner, Toumanova—have special and personal attributes to bring to a classic which belongs to the ballerinas of all eras. But of this host, Cuba's Alicia Alonso is one of the best.

The Alonso career started modestly enough. At the age of eight, she was sent to dancing school (the ballet school of the Sociedad Pro-Arte Musical in Havana) to acquire poise and grace. A professional career for the daughter of a socially eminent family? Out of the question. But talent took a hand in the decision. Critics found her the most promising student in Cuba and such a one could hardly be stopped by mere social conventions or even by motherhood. She married young—her daughter was born before she was sixteen—but neither she nor Fernando thought that a promising student should refuse the promise of a career.

The young couple came to New York and the ballerina-to-be continued her studies at the School of American Ballet, with Anatole Vilzak (an artist of the Russian Imperial Theater and a star of the Diaghilev ballet) and Alexandra Fedorova (also a graduate of the Imperial school). With the coming of paying jobs, Alicia's father had to be told (her mother was in on the secret), but so good were the critical reviews that he forgave his disobedient daughter and placed his blessings upon her and her new life as a professional dancer.

The blessings were not misplaced, for not only did Alicia go on to fame as *prima ballerina* of Ballet Theatre but she and her husband founded the Ballet Alicia Alonso (she appears with it whenever her Ballet Theatre commitments permit), which has had the sponsorship of the Cuban Ministry of Education and which has toured the Latin American world with considerable success. And finally, to a girl who was not supposed to perform professionally, came government recognition in the form of the Carlos Manuel de Cespedes Medal, Cuba's highest civilian honor, carrying with it the title of "Dama."

Although her Giselle has been hailed in the United States, in Central and South America, and in Europe, Alonso is not a one-role ballerina. She has mastered such classics as *Swan Lake, Les Sylphides, Aurora's Wedding* (called *Princess Aurora* in Ballet Theatre), and a variety of *pas de deux:* "Bluebird," "Black Swan," *Don Quixote, Nutcracker.* In all, she is regal and gracious as the ballerina tradition demands, but, like Markova, she brings much of her own

182

ALICIA ALONSO IN
"LES SYLPHIDES"

personality to bear upon the interpretation of even the most academic assignments.

The present as well as the past employs her talents and thus she has lent her services to the contemporary choreographer. In Balanchine's *Theme and Variations*, for example, she is quite without equal. He has exploited both the length and the extension of her leg in unfolding movements of the utmost loveliness and in a slow-motion *adagio* which finds her supported by an entire *corps* of girls. He has used her appealing femininity in yielding actions which press her close to the body of her cavalier, and he has employed her precision in the most delicate of steps, which tread the stage as gently as a lithographed Taglioni skimming across a world of petals.

This same classicist, however, can convey harshness and writhing evil, as she does in Tudor's *Undertow* in the role of Ate (which she created), goddess of infatuation, mischief, and guilt. A more frightening characterization—slimy, unclean, as hypnotic as a snake—would be hard to imagine. She has also danced the part of Lizzie Borden in Agnes de Mille's superb *Fall River Legend* and actually danced in its first presentation. Although the part was designed for Nora Kaye, illness intervened, and Alonso, stepping in at the last moment, proved herself an actress, not an actress-dancer in a class with Kaye, but a proficient one nonetheless.

She has been and can be captivating as Juliet in the Tudor ballet, believable and glorious as Taglioni in *Pas de Quatre*, poignant and shy in *On Stage!*, hilarious as the Italian ballerina in *Gala Performance*, impressive as the Other Woman in *Lilac Garden*, wild and fiery as the ravished woman in Herbert Ross's *Caprichos*. But over all shines the aristocratic presence of the classic ballerina. The Latin temperament of Catherine de Medici is born anew in the Latin fire

184

of a New World ballerina; the courtly elegancies of Lafontaine and Prévost are revived in her proud bearing; Taglioni's lightness and Legnani's virtuosity, Pavlova's unreality, and, in fact, the bequests of centuries of ballerinas exert their influences, large and small, strongly or fleetingly, on a Cuban ballerina who belongs to the world of dance.

Alonso is not, of course, the alpha and the omega of ballet. There are other ballerinas—some her equals, some her superiors, some her inferiors—who share in the awful burden of the star tradition. Four supreme artists—Danilova, Markova, Kaye, Maria Tallchief—who are particularly close to the hearts of the American public are treated elsewhere in this book, but there are yet others who deserve mention because of their achievement or their promise, their beauty or their technical skill, their artistry or their popularity, because they can make the grade or because they partially failed to do so.

NANA GOLLNER IN
"GALA PERFORMANCE"

Nana Gollner, contemporary ballerina, the first modern American girl to achieve the rank of prima ballerina *in a European company. As a ballerina with Ballet Theatre during the 1940's, she enjoyed success in such ballets as* Swan Lake, Giselle, La Fille Mal Gardée, *and* Undertow *(in which she created the role of Medusa).*

A case in point is Nana Gollner, potentially one of the greatest ballerinas of our time. Weakened by infantile paralysis when a child, Nana studied ballet to bring strength to her muscles, and so well did she succeed that she became one of the strongest of dancers, able to stand *sur la pointe* barefoot, equipped to perform any movement assigned to her, wholly durable. She was the first contemporary American to attain the rank of *prima ballerina* in a foreign company, and she brought her physical strength and beauty, her prodigious technique, and her not always dependable artistry to an array of ballet companies, including the American Ballet, the Blum and De Basil Ballet Russe, the Original Ballet Russe, Ballet Theatre, and other smaller units, mainly those under the direction of herself and her husband (Paul Petroff).

But the Gollner career has been hampered, as the ballet follower knows, by that undependable artistry, by a feeling that sometimes she likes to dance and sometimes she doesn't. At her best, she gives breath-taking performances of *Giselle* or *Swan Lake*, performances which are technically and stylistically flawless, yet tinged with warmth and dramatic passion. Again, she can be, in these very same ballets, cold as ice, and although audiences have rarely found her sloppy technically, they have seen her appear wholly indifferent to the business at hand.

187

As she commences to slip (and let us hope that this is temporary) from her place of importance in the ballerina world, she leaves her many admirers with some wonderful memories: her best Swan Queens and Giselles; her delicious girl in *La Fille Mal Gardée*, the frightening Medusa (a role which she created) in *Undertow*, her richly funny enactment of the cold, haughty, statuesque, almost architectural Italian ballerina in *Gala Performance*, the perfect aplomb of her dancing in *Aurora*, the most beautiful *développés* in the world, unfolding and floating skyward; the surprise of her left-footedness (most dancer's turn to the right), which caused her to do traveling turns on her left foot or use the left as the whip in *fouettés* (when partnered, she turned to the right!); the beauty of her body; the many wonders of Gollner at her best.

The Gollner trouble was that she was not at her best often enough and so a fine ballerina and a potentially great artist never quite achieved that towering stature which belongs only to the few.

Mia Slavenska, contemporary ballerina, born in Yugoslavia. First seen in America as a ballerina with the Ballet Russe de Monte Carlo in the late 1930's. In 1947, she founded her own ballet group. She is a skilled interpreter of traditional roles and has created parts in new ballets.

In Mia Slavenska, America (and the world) possesses a completely dependable ballerina, one who can be counted upon to give fine performances at all times. At the age of five, in her native Yugoslavia, she was already a child star at the Zagreb National Opera

188

and by the time she was a veteran of twelve, she was ready for a partner, a concert debut, and touring. With this stage experience behind her, further ballet studies with Egorova, Preobrajenska, and Kchessinskaya in Paris, *modern dance* training, a prize for her participation in the Berlin Dance Olympics, and appearances with the Ballet Russe de Monte Carlo and other organizations in Europe, she was ready for an international career.

America first saw her in the late 1930's, when she danced as a ballerina with the Ballet Russe de Monte Carlo. In her comparatively long association with this company—before she founded her own ballet group in 1947—she created new roles and assumed the stellar parts in *Giselle, Swan Lake, The Magic Swan* (an act from the full-length *Le Lac des Cygnes*), *Coppélia, Nutcracker, Les Sylphides,* and *Scheherazade,* to name but a handful of the ballets she has mastered.

It is quite unlikely that Mia Slavenska has ever given a careless performance. She has, in the past, overacted and sold her tricks (such as her remarkable balance) to the audience, and in comedies she leans toward coyness, but she is every inch a ballerina, an exciting star. But she is not often a luminous artist. Her dancing of classical parts is correct, conventional. In *Coppélia* she is gay and sparkling; in *Giselle* she is tragic; in *Nutcracker* she is lyrical. In these and in other ballets, she is always fine and, occasionally, inspired and inspiring, but in the main she does not reveal so much as she presents. In handsome fashion, she presents her own personal beauty, her perfect technique, and all the outlines and some of the substance of the ballets in which she appears. She is a performer, rather than an interpreter or a creator, and in this capacity she is a ballerina, one of the best in the business.

189

Rosella Hightower, contemporary American ballerina. She has danced with the Ballet Russe de Monte Carlo, Ballet Theatre, the Original Ballet Russe, and the Marquis de Cuevas' Grand Ballet. She is even better known abroad than in her own country.

In Rosella Hightower, America has a ballerina of which it may be proud. Like the Tallchiefs, Maria and Marjorie, Indian blood flows in her veins and virtuosity springs from her limbs. In her career with the Ballet Russe de Monte Carlo, Ballet Theatre, the Original Ballet Russe, and the Marquis de Cuevas' Grand Ballet, she has met and conquered all sorts of challenges. Her first *Giselle* took place at the Metropolitan Opera House after only a few hours of rehearsal, and it would not have come off so well as it did if it had not been for the kind and authoritative direction of Anton Dolin and Hightower's own readiness for whatever came her way. It was not and could not be a finished characterization, but it was a great performance by a girl with the stuff of the ballerina in her.

And today, Rosella Hightower is a star of international repute, as admired in Europe as in her own America. She, too, is a Swan Queen, a Swanhilda, a Sugar Plum Fairy, and a Black Swan, but she is also a comedian (*Graduation Ball*) and a fine dramatic actress (*Sebastian*). As a matter of fact, one of the memorable moments in the theater of dance is Hightower's dance of the bewitched and dying maiden in *Sebastian*, for here is consummate control of muscle energy, perfection in the communication of a dramatic situation.

Marjorie Tallchief, American ballerina and sister of Maria Tall-chief. Although she has danced with Ballet Theatre and the Original Ballet Russe, she is best known as a ballerina with the Marquis de Cuevas' Grand Ballet, a company which performs mainly in Europe.

Paralleling the Hightower career is that of Marjorie Tallchief, Maria's sister and the third American ballerina with Indian ancestry to boast of. After basic training with Ballet Theatre and the Original Ballet Russe, Marjorie joined the Marquis de Cuevas' Grand Ballet, where she has shared many ballerina roles with Hightower. In profile, one can hardly say whether it is Maria or Marjorie on stage, and their dancing—sharp, quick, glowing with banked fires—is much alike. Marjorie, the younger of the Tallchiefs, is not yet her sister's equal (although she and her husband, George Skibine, have produced twins!), but she is a potential rival, albeit a friendly one.

Among the other junior ballerinas, one must certainly list Mary Ellen Moylan, formerly of Ballet Theatre, and the same company's Melissa Hayden, the New York City Ballet's Janet Reed, Tanaquil LeClercq, and Diana Adams. Moylan, proficient in many roles, has one great ballet in which she has never been equaled, Balanchine's *Ballet Imperial*. In this masterpiece, she moves with unbelievable swiftness and precision, touching her characterization with just the right degree of amusing and bemused hauteur, behaving as an imperial ballerina should behave, mirroring in her actions every detail of musical accent and nuance. At times, she is a spotty dancer, sometimes magnificent as the Swan Queen, as Aurora, as the Wili queen of *Giselle*, as the pastoral heroine of *Constantia*, as the ballerina in *Theme and Variations*, and as the cat-girl in *Les Demoiselles de la Nuit*, but again, contrarily, she is tense, uneasy, off balance, unhappy in these very same roles. A ballerina, no doubt about it, but one still seeking self-assurance and dependable controls.

There is no one else in the dance world quite like the lovely Janet Reed. She is neither a virtuoso nor a glittering stage figure, but she is a very special artist who contributes much-needed sweetness, innocence, and childlike delicacy to ballet. She is, of course, a highly proficient dancer, quite prepared to dance difficult *enchaînements*, but her particular value lies in the charm, the wit, the communicable good nature, even the wistful sadness she commands. In *Serenade*, in the beautiful reverie which is *Mother Goose Suite*, in the happy humor of *Cakewalk*, in the wild and unexpected kinetics of *Pied Piper*, in the bounding conclusion of *Bourrée Fantasque* and in countless other ballets, Janet Reed is irreplaceable. One does not often become excited over her dancing and one does not find in her the regal bearing of the classic ballerina, but one falls in love with her dancing and, incidentally, with the ballerina herself.

As a ballerina with the San Francisco Opera Ballet, Dance Players, Ballet Theatre, and the New York City Ballet, she has danced everything from a full-length *Swan Lake* to *Fancy Free*, creating along the way a raft of new roles, almost all of them instantaneous successes. She has been a tramp in the *Judgment of Paris*, a restless wife in *Tally-Ho!*, a mischievous teen-age sister in *Pillar of Fire*, and a re-creation of Cerito herself in *Pas de Quatre*. And if there is a temptation to omit Janet Reed's name from a roster of ballerinas, it is simply because she is not spectacular, simply because she is not a show-off, but, rather, an unobtrusive, modest, and quietly great artist of dance.

Tanaquil LeClercq is a young colt; Melissa Hayden, a gleaming sword; Diana Adams, a melody. None is quite yet a full-fledged, mature ballerina, although each has assumed ballerina and major character parts with considerable success. One of Adams' finest roles is that of Iseult in Frederick Ashton's *Picnic at Tintagel*, but she is also exquisite in Balanchine's *Symphonie Concertante*, which she dances with LeClercq as co-ballerina.

In this *Symphonie*, LeClercq, too, is impressive. While Adams' dark beauty and richly flowing movements reflect the musical patterns of the viola, LeClercq's brightness and sharper actions pursue the phrases of the violin. In *The Age of Anxiety*, she is wholly appealing, and her youthful lankiness is transformed by poetry of motion into communicable wistfulness in Robbins' strange *Ballade*. Furthermore, she is a fine comic, as her zany activities in *Bourrée Fantasque* testify.

Of the three, Hayden is nearest true ballerina status, for no one can be indifferent to her presence. Dynamic power (she has more than almost any other young ballet artist) and technical authority are manifest in her dancing, and it must seem to everyone that no one could replace her as the girl-warrior of *The Duel* or as the lecherous, abandoned, clawing figure of Profane Love in *Illuminations*.

There are other contestants—near-ballerinas and soloists—for the rank of ballerina, but they will have to struggle for, wait for, and pray for that unpredictable moment when, as one of them walks onto the stage, the audience, with brightening eyes and quicker heartbeat, murmurs "Ballerina!"

QUEEN OF THE SADLER'S WELLS

Margot Fonteyn, contemporary English dancer and prima ballerina of the Sadler's Wells Ballet. She is noted for her roles in full-length productions of The Sleeping Beauty, Swan Lake, *and* Sylvia. *Fonteyn, through the tours of the Sadler's Wells Ballet, has become almost as popular in America as in England.*

MARGOT FONTEYN IN "THE SLEEPING BEAUTY"

Americans are so proud of their ballerinas—native, adopted, borrowed—that they occasionally forget that Europe, which created the ballerina in the first place, has its contemporary contenders for supremacy in the ballerina league. Of those artists who maintain headquarters in their own lands beyond the seas, none is more greatly admired nor better loved than England's Margot Fonteyn, *prima ballerina* of the Sadler's Wells Ballet.

When she made her American debut with the Sadler's Wells at the Metropolitan Opera House in 1950, her name was unknown (except for balletomanes) to Americans. As far as local audiences were concerned, the star of the company was the second ballerina, Moira Shearer, for her name had become practically a household word in America because of the success of her movie, *The Red Shoes.*

Before the season at the Metropolitan opened, theater-goers quite understandably preferred to buy tickets for those programs in which Shearer was scheduled to appear. But once Fonteyn had danced—it was the opening-night performance—it was apparent to all that Fonteyn and not Shearer was the *prima ballerina.*

Not even movie glory could obscure the light of a stage star. Everyone heaved a sigh, for the management had done its best to publicize Fonteyn as the *prima* and Shearer as the second. And Shearer herself was relieved when the public accepted the proper sequence of rank. Unworried was the always modest Fonteyn.

For Fonteyn, dance seems to be almost a religion; a career, the act of dedication. She has worked hard all her life, and if chance favored her, talent and discipline and devotion made her quick rise to fame wholly warranted. In a sense she is the most thoroughly "home-product" ballerina that England has produced, for, unlike

Markova, she had most of her training with the Sadler's Wells School and her career has been almost exclusively linked with the Sadler's Wells company.

She was born in England (1919), was reared in England, China, and America, and returned permanently to her homeland in 1932 for a continuation of her ballet studies under Astafieva (Markova's teacher) and with Ninette de Valois, then associated with the Vic-Wells Ballet and later to become director of the Sadler's Wells Ballet. By 1934, she was ready for professional appearances and joined the company as a *corps de ballet* girl. Before the year was out, she had assumed solo parts, and the following year, when Markova left, she was already being groomed for and tested in the roles that Markova herself had danced. By 1940, Margot Fonteyn was not only the company's first dancer, but also the most popular ballerina in England.

It cannot be denied that Markova's departing and the wartime years, with their dearth of art exchanges, gave Fonteyn her opportunity, but she was, in every way, worthy of it, and with her flowering, English ballet came of age.

In Margot Fonteyn, the characteristics of English classical dancing are embodied, for she is lyrical in style, meticulous in movement, somewhat reserved but gracious, skillful and deliberate in miming. Her phrasing, musically, is also perfect. Thus she represents the major attributes of England's version of classical dancing, and thus she differs from the American ballerina and America's concept of classicism, a conception which tends to stress speed and power (as well as meticulousness), dynamic variety, dramatic accent, and rhythm (with all its degrees of accent and pulsations) as opposed to simple recognition of beat and measure and phrase.

197

Traditional mime, which can be so eloquent and lovely when performed by a Fonteyn, baffles or embarrasses many an American artist.

But differences in national styles cannot destroy appreciation, for differences enrich the whole, and when Fonteyn dances, no American in his right mind could fail to see in her one of the great ballerinas of our day. Take her Aurora in *The Sleeping Beauty*. Here is a girl-princess, protected but unspoiled, regal but childlike. She runs lightly through the ballet, shedding radiance upon all the figures in the dance and sending the warm glow of beauty across the footlights. She ripens as the ballet unfolds, growing from a playful little girl into a poised princess. And the poise is given its exposition in dance in the famed "Rose Adagio," which calls upon the ballerina to stand long and easily on point as she receives the obeisances, the tributes, the roses of her cavaliers. Only a fairytale princess would do this; only a ballerina could do it with consummate ease.

In *Swan Lake* (the full-length production), Fonteyn's dramatic abilities and her skill in altering classical movements through harder accents and sharper line are given greater scope. The dual role of Odette-Odile requires this shift of accent, for as Odette, the Swan Queen, she is a heroine, imperial but sweet and good and loving, but as Odile, the daughter of an evil magician, she must attempt to impersonate the Queen of the Swans to the degree that the Prince-lover is fooled but not the audience.

Thus, in the *adagio* for the Prince and the Queen of the Swans, we see a tender and lyrical figure dancing her tragedy and her romance and her hope. But in the "Black Swan" *pas de deux*, the figure of the woman, although still desirable, pretending to amorousness, is hard and glittering; her protestations of love are teasing rather than inviting; the patterns of her dance are like a web of steel wound around the unsuspecting Prince; and the thirty-two *fouettés* flash their message of arrogant and inexorable power.

On the strength of her performances in *Swan Lake* as produced in four acts by the Sadler's Wells Ballet, the American is tempted to say that Fonteyn is the supreme contemporary interpreter of the Swan Queen. America, however, has seen no other full-length productions of this classic, and never its own stars in the challenging double role. Until such comparisons can be made (Fonteyn is the acknowledged superior of other Sadler's Wells ballerinas in this part), the Odette-Odile of Margot Fonteyn wears the crown of achievement.

This ballerina, however, has other fine characterizations upon which her enviable reputation is based. Not only does she excel as Odette-Odile and as Princess Aurora (considered by most authorities as her finest enactment), but she is also admired for her performances in *Giselle, Nutcracker, Coppélia, Le Spectre de la Rose,* and other ballets which have endured the tests of years of performances.

In 1953 and 1954, when the Sadler's Wells Ballet again toured America, audiences saw Fonteyn in a new role in a new evening-length classical ballet. This was *Sylvia,* an old nineteenth-century ballet to the continuously popular music of Delibes, totally re-choreographed by Frederick Ashton, the Sadler's Wells Ballet's chief choreographer. In *Sylvia,* the most opulent of the English company's productions, Fonteyn enjoyed still further success, and small wonder, for in it she had a part that displayed her scope as an actress as well as her range as a dancer.

"It's a pretty silly story," says Fonteyn, "but the leading role is the kind that ballerinas dream about and seldom get." On both points of comment, most onlookers are agreed that Fonteyn is right. The plot, an extremely involved one, has to do with a beautiful huntress (Sylvia), a shepherd who loves her, the goddess Diana in whose entourage Sylvia belongs, the god of love, a villain, and other mortal and celestial beings. But all the activities in which these assorted characters become engaged are centered around Sylvia herself and require an array of dramatic reactions in dance.

During the course of *Sylvia*, Fonteyn is called upon to be a flashing warrior maiden, a frightened girl, a pretended wanton, a haughty female, a lady in love, a queenly individual, and variations thereof. Each of these aspects of character naturally requires acting skill, but since *Sylvia* is a ballet and not a spoken drama, it follows that different dance accents, rhythms, and styles are expected of the ballerina. It is hardly surprising, then, that Fonteyn finds *Sylvia* a "dream role," and because she is able to make a dream come true, American audiences have found that Fonteyn herself is pretty much of a dream in one of ballet's most demanding parts.

Britain's lovely dance star also dances in nontraditional ballets. She has been the cat-girl in *Les Demoiselles de la Nuit*, a barefoot dancer in *Dante Sonata*, a poignant Ophelia in a dance version of *Hamlet*, the radiant heroine of *Daphnis and Chloë*, a Spanish dancer in *The Three-Cornered Hat*, and the classical, swift Queen of the Air in the ballet composed by Frederick Ashton in honor of the coronation of Queen Elizabeth II, *Homage to the Queen*.

More than natural talent was needed to lift Fonteyn to her present point of eminence in the ballet world. Not only did she study long and hard as a child dance student in classrooms in China, America, and England, but she has also continued her studies with a self-discipline which amazes her colleagues. No matter how many performances and rehearsals are on her schedule, she never misses a class, for Fonteyn is a perfectionist. Even her most successful roles are studied and restudied in an unceasing effort to improve characterizations which, to the onlooker, seem perfect already.

Before a performance of *The Sleeping Beauty*, a ballet she has danced more than a hundred times, it is not unusual to find Fonteyn going over passages in her variations, polishing details of action. This last-minute and seemingly unnecessary rehearsing is done because the ballerina is determined to present, at each fresh performance, a finer Princess Aurora than she has ever presented before, and it is also possible that by occupying herself in such a way, she is able to dispel to a degree the nervousness which attacks her before the curtain rises. For Fonteyn, as celebrated as she is, succumbs to a case of nerves before she dances, a state shared by the majority of stars of dance.

Humbleness, friendliness, and generosity are traits which Fonteyn possesses and which endear her to friends, acquaintances, and dancing colleagues in the company. She is eager to help newcomers to the company feel at home not only in their roles but also as individuals. Off-stage, she retains the dignity associated with the many aristocratic parts she portrays, but there is no haughtiness, no coldness in this attitude, for her frequent smile is genuine and her laughing, mischievous eyes reveal a girl who likes nothing better than a joke, particularly when she herself is the butt of the joke.

Her humble attitude was best demonstrated on the occasion of the Sadler's Wells Ballet's American debut at the Metropolitan Opera House. When the curtain fell on *The Sleeping Beauty*, there were cheers, many of them for Fonteyn, a ballerina whom an American audience had just discovered for itself. But Fonteyn refused to take a solo bow before the great gold curtains of the Met. It took the urging of the entire company to get her to go forth for the tribute due her. Later, she explained her reason for not wanting to take a solo call: "I didn't feel it was my night. I felt it was the company's."

Not the least of the ballerina's qualities is courage. In the early 1950's, Fonteyn was taken desperately ill with a disease diagnosed as a form of diphtheria. Her recovery was necessarily slow, but the most frightening part came when she commenced to practice again and discovered that, as she put it, "my balance seemed to desert me." There were many who wondered whether she would ever be able to resume her career, but work and determination saw her through the most difficult year of her life and she returned to the Sadler's Wells to become an even greater artist than she had been before.

On her return to America in 1953 with the Sadler's Wells, those familiar with her dancing thought they recognized a new radiance, a new sensitivity, a new vitality. Martha Graham, America's leading modern dancer, who is a great admirer of Fonteyn, explained the new Fonteyn qualities by saying, "It is as if she were dancing a prayer of thanksgiving, as if she were one who had looked death in the face and had miraculously been restored to the wonder of life. To a dancer, you see, a life without dancing would be death and Fonteyn, apparently, came close to just such a death."

FROM ENGLAND, FRANCE, RUSSIA

Moira Shearer, Scottish dancer, is a ballerina with the Sadler's Wells Ballet and a motion picture star. Her first big movie hit was The Red Shoes, *and her successful ballets have included most of the classics in the Sadler's Wells repertory and such comedy ballets as* A Wedding Bouquet.

Margot Fonteyn, respected and loved as she is by American audiences, is not the only ballerina from overseas who has aroused the interest, either by visit or through rumor, of American balletomanes. Other English ballerinas and dance stars of France and Russia (ballet dancers in other European nations are less well publicized) must be granted their places in any chronicle treating with ballerinas. Of this particular group, perhaps the most universally popular is Margot Fonteyn's junior colleague, Moira Shearer.

Shearer, who shuttles back and forth between theater ballet and movie ballet, may not have achieved equality with Fonteyn, but she is without question a ballerina. Her dancing is as bright as her red hair, and it follows that her movements are quick and alive with energy and dash. Her Princess Aurora is lovely, more regal and less wistful than Fonteyn's, and her Cinderella in Frederick Ashton's full-length ballet of the same name is just as all of us have dreamed this fairytale girl to be.

Although Shearer is completely at ease in such traditional ballets as *The Sleeping Beauty, Swan Lake,* or *Giselle* (and she has been recognized as one of the best of many Giselles), her comic gifts are so enchanting that one can never forget her cavortings in the rollicking *Façade* or as the pleasantly mad Julia in *A Wedding Bouquet*. As Julia, Shearer is accompanied not only by music but also by the curious and humorous lines of the poetess Gertrude Stein, and in one hilarious section, as she flings herself into postures and patterns of hopeless abandon, one hears the orator reading a Stein line which says, "She has no plans for the winter." And by Julia's distracted expression, we may be pretty certain that she has no plans for any time of year.

In almost every one of her roles, Shearer gives accent to the dramatic as well as to the pure dance elements of ballet. It is not surprising, then, that a movie career of considerable magnitude has been successfully launched. Obviously Moira Shearer was not picked for her beauty alone or for her photogenic qualities. These were helpful attributes, but her acting range was even more important if she was to become a motion picture star and not merely a photographed dancer.

Until *The Red Shoes* came her way, Shearer was hardly known outside of England and in a few European cities. Here was a Scotswoman who had studied dancing under Mme. Nicholas Legat, trained at the Sadler's Wells Ballet School, made her debut with the International Ballet, joined the Sadler's Wells company the next year as a *corps de ballet* girl, and risen to the rank of ballerina by 1944. With *The Red Shoes*, she became better known than Fonteyn herself, better known than the ballet company in which she was a ballerina. Indeed, she became an international star by way of moving pictures.

The Red Shoes demanded the services of an actress-dancer. In the story, Shearer had to play the on-stage, off-stage life of the dancer,

MOIRA
SHEARER
IN
"CINDERELLA"

and it was her difficult task to communicate that strange dedication to unbelievable hardship and ephemeral beauty which the ballerina must possess if she is to win and retain a post of dance stardom. In the long ballet within the movie story, Shearer's natural beauties of movement were enhanced by the magic of the camera, which could transform action of normal speed into hypnotic slow motion or accelerate it to a pitch of dizzying excitement. The camera, through close-ups, could explore the expressivity of face or hand or dancing foot, and it could break past the boundaries of stage space with visions of figures dancing up to the clouds or skirting the horizon. This was a new kind of ballet magic, and the lovely Moira Shearer, ballerina, was its focus.

With Fonteyn heading the Sadler's Wells, Shearer lending her talents to both stage and screen, and the traveling Markova returning to her homeland from season to season, English ballet has been fortunate. But, always, tomorrow must be considered, and so England and its native ballet schools and companies have continued to groom young artists for the rank of ballerina. Beautiful Violetta Elvin; Svetlana Beriosova, long-limbed and mysterious; Elaine Fifield, piquant; the handsome and technically accurate Rowena Jackson; and smiling, appealing Nadia Nerina are among the contestants for ballet stardom in the English arena of ballet action.

Across the narrow channel from England, the French, whose historic place in the building of ballet is universally recognized, continue their contributions to an art which has now become international. Of the several ballerinas who have danced with the famed company of the Paris Opéra or in independent ballet organizations, the three best known to American audiences are Yvette Chauviré, Renée Jeanmaire, and Colette Marchand.

Chauviré was first seen and admired by Americans in a brief engagement which the Paris Opéra Ballet had in New York, but later the country as a whole was to see her when she appeared as guest star with the Ballet Russe de Monte Carlo in its extensive tours.

But although Chauviré made an impression upon the dance public, she achieved nothing like the popular successes experienced by Jeanmaire and Marchand, who first performed in America as principal dancers in Roland Petit's modern, racy, and highly theatrical Ballets de Paris and who later went on to movie stardom.

It didn't take Americans very long to speak of Marchand as "Les Legs," a title conferred upon her by an admiring reviewer, and Jeanmaire scored an instant hit in the title part of Petit's sultry and violent ballet version of the opera *Carmen*.

Because of the theatrical modernity of the ballets in which they appeared first to the American public, because they sing and act as well as dance, because movies and musical comedies have almost succeeded in cornering their time and talents, it is sometimes hard to think of Jeanmaire and Marchand as ballerinas. But ballerinas they are, and no matter what their theatrical assignments may be, they continue to study as all ballerinas study and to maintain an unswerving devotion to an ancient art which their ballerina ancestors—Lafontaine, Camargo, Guimard—helped to build for them.

Galina Ulanova, contemporary Russian ballerina, is recognized as the top ballet star in the Soviet Union.

Unlike Fonteyn or Jeanmaire, who are free to visit theaters around the globe, there is one curtain which rarely rises on Galina Ulanova, People's Artist of the Republic and the Soviet Union's top ballerina.

That curtain is, of course, the Iron Curtain, and so audiences of the Western world may know of her dancing only through motion pictures, through a brief appearance in Italy on a festival series, and through words. The words of writers—Russian writers and those foreigners who have been able to see Ulanova in her homeland— make it clear that she is looked upon as the most celebrated artist of her country. It is agreed that she is primarily a lyricist, that her dancing recalls descriptions of Taglioni, that her greatest role is in *Giselle*, and that although other Russian ballerinas (Olga Lepeshinskaya, for example) may be more spectacular and have more virtuosity, it is Ulanova who makes stage magic.

Memories of Pavlova and legends of Taglioni appear to be reborn in that incredible lightness which is Ulanova's special gift. We are told that the air, rather than the ground, is her dancing site. Seemingly, she soars without effort, flutters delicately as if guided by a gentle breeze, poises so gently upon a *pointe* that one is hardly aware of the contact between foot and earth. Finally, it is said that her movements are flowing, so fluid that they remind one of a song, a murmur, an unbroken elegy. For sadness, too, touches upon her dancing. She can be gay, but it is a gaiety tinged with sorrow. Off-stage, she is drab, a trifle stooped, wistful, more like a musing poetess than a glittering ballerina, and although the stage brings forth her vitality and her beauty, something of the dreaming poet remains as if to give sad comment upon the aching sorrow of romance.

The films of her which have come out of Russia suggest that all that has been said must be true. But these movies tease rather than inform. All of them, including the comparatively recent *Grand Concert*, in which she dances episodes from *Romeo and Juliet*, give

GALINA ULANOVA
IN "GISELLE"

us glimpses only. One can see that she is truly light, that her body flows as easily as the draperies which flutter about it, that a delicate wistfulness pervades her dancing.

Like her colleagues—Marina Semyonova, cool and classical; Lepeshinskaya, effervescent and flashing; Maya Plisetkaya, sharp and full of virtuosity—Ulanova holds her chest high, bends her

GALINA ULANOVA IN
"ROMEO AND JULIET"

instep (like the arc of a bow) over her toe, and reveals a steely strength beneath a relaxed surface. As far as one can judge, she is a traditionalist, a follower of the style of romantic ballet, but just as Markova infuses her own personality into traditional roles supposedly set by time and custom, so does Ulanova color familiar movements through her own degrees of stress and softness, through the tilt of the head or arch of the back, through the curve or straightness or flow of an arm.

What her enactment of *Giselle* is like can only be conjectured. Certainly it would be an ideal ballet for one who seems frail and sad, for a lyric artist, for a dancer whose aerial qualities make her seem magical, out of this world. Those who have seen her say that in this, her own favorite ballet, she is quite without equal in Russia and, perhaps, in the world. But until that Iron Curtain which separates this artist from a vaster world of dance is raised, we cannot be certain just where Ulanova belongs in the roster of the world's great ballerinas.

In her forties (she was born in 1912 into a family of dancers), Ulanova has contributed new and personal performing values to the art of ballet. She has not, as far as is known, invented any new steps, created ballets, wrought innovations. But if she has not been a Camargo, a Sallé, a Taglioni, or a Kaye, she has surely renewed and revitalized for Russia the finest traditions of classical dancing. In a land which despises the aristocrat, she is a Queen, for not only does she dance the Queen of the Swans in *Swan Lake*, the noble Juliet, and one loved by a Prince in *Cinderella*, but that regal bearing instituted by Catherine de Medici is to be found in the highly held head, the proud carriage, the elegance of the communists' favorite artist.

MARIA TALLCHIEF
IN "FIREBIRD"

Seventeen

AMERICAN BALLERINA

Maria Tallchief, contemporary American ballerina of Osage Indian heritage, appeared in 1942 with the Ballet Russe de Monte Carlo for the first time. In 1947, she appeared as guest ballerina at the Paris Opéra, and later in the same year she became star of the new Ballet Society, an organization which soon became the New York City Ballet. One of the greatest technicians in the history of ballet, Tallchief has excelled in ballets choreographed by Balanchine.

While Catherine de Medici, Queen of France, and her ladies of the court were residing in vast edifices of stone, Maria Tallchief's ancestors were moving beneath the great vault of the sky or the soaring arches made by the branches of mighty trees. Catherine and her ladies in their stiff, heavy gowns and with their feet pinched into shoes made their slow and stately way across smooth and polished floors. In the New World, a bronze-skinned people moved their unencumbered bodies freely, pressed their bare or softly shod feet against the earth, and danced, not merely for their own pleasure but for their gods.

Almost four hundred years were to pass before these two distinct heritages could meet and mate successfully in the theater of dance, and once they were united, it was not difficult to see that there were and always had been points in common: beauty and elegance of bearing, aristocracy of mien, rhythmic harmony, etiquette, respect for pattern, love of movement. There were differences, major ones, but those Indian qualities which Maria Tallchief elected to bring with her to an art form inaugurated by Catherine de Medici infused the art of the ballerina with new fire and strength.

The New York City Ballet's *prima ballerina* does not wear moccasins in place of toe slippers, nor has she discarded the *tutu* and tiara for beaded deerskin and feathers. She is every inch the classical ballerina. Indeed, her movements are so precise that they could serve as living models of that dance technique developed and perfected by such of her artistic forebears as Camargo, Taglioni, Legnani, and Karsavina. Yet there is something more to her dancing than academic perfection. Is it mere imagining, or does her leg dart to its balletic destination with the swift beauty of an accurately propeled arrow? Does not her body, in some positions, mirror the fine, resilient arch of the bow? And her feet! Yes, they are in toe slippers, but they are incredibly strong and unhesitating in their pursuit of those choreographic trails which lead to dance excitement.

Her face, with its high cheekbones and generous mouth, is an Indian face, and her almost boyishly slim, agile, and powerful body reproduces the physical majesty of her people. On stage, with her head held high and her spine erect, she is an Indian princess, as aristocratic as Catherine of France or the Queen of the Swans, whose story she so often dances.

Primitive fire and savage splendor may, at first glance, seem to be attributes more suitable to tribal dances than to the ballet, yet Tallchief has used them effectively, wisely, and, no doubt, instinctively. For there is latent fire in the passion of the Swan Queen and there is primitive intensity in the gypsy-fairy figure from *Le Baiser de la Fée*. And if savage splendor has a place in classical ballet, it is surely in *Firebird*, one of Tallchief's most illustrious characterizations. These special qualities, properly adapted, may even serve

214

classical, storyless ballet. Primal energy can give flashing speed to a *pirouette*, and the primitive impetus to seek outlet in dance can certainly bring a flush of life to the coldest of academic patterns. Thus Tallchief, in herself, represents a fusion of traditional method and style with the natural lust for danced action.

The Tallchief heritage is one thing; her training is quite another. Although she was born on an Osage reservation in Oklahoma, she wants it known that her home was a house and not a tepee. Her father is an Indian; her mother, of Scotch descent; her grandmother, Eliza Tall Chief; her great-grandfather, Chief Big Heart. Of this heritage she is, of course, justly proud, but her relation to Indian ways is tenuous at best. She recalls little of Indian ceremonies in the reservation town of Fairfax, but she remembers clearly the piano lessons and the ballet classes given by an itinerant teacher.

As a matter of fact, the Tallchiefs thought they had a prodigy on their hands. No one in the family (except her father, who played the saxophone) had shown any remarkable musical bent; yet, at three, little Maria was playing the piano with surprising skill and considerable gusto. Ballet was of minor importance, at least to the parents, but talent in dancing was also manifest in the little girl. When only five, Maria could have been seen in recital spinning endlessly on point while she waved the American flag to the tune of "The Stars and Stripes Forever." Why she had any feet worthy of the name left to her after this shattering experience, she does not know, but survive such dangerous training she did, and now she cries out disapprovingly against any teacher who would let a child use toe slippers before the age of eight.

With "Stars and Stripes" behind her, Maria and the family departed for California, and a new period of training in music and dance commenced. Her parents, unimpressed with the flag-waving episode and a number performed to "Glowworm," urged her to concentrate upon her music, and this she did, but ballet was not wholly neglected. By the time she was twelve or thirteen, solo recitals on the piano and performances of concertos with local orchestral groups were not infrequent. A musician's career seemed ordained, but Maria had other ideas, and at one of her recitals she devoted half of the program to piano music and the second half to dancing. The omen was clear; a potential ballerina was going to eliminate a potential concert pianist.

At fifteen, the die was cast. The place: Hollywood Bowl. The presentation: *Chopin Concerto*. But this time Maria was not piano soloist, for the work was offered as a ballet and in the dancing cast were Chief Big Heart's great-granddaughter and another unknown teen-ager, Cyd Charisse, later to become a movie star.

The Indian feet which had defied the destructive elements of bad teaching back in Oklahoma were now being retrained, the faults unlearned, and correct ballet methods mastered. Ernest Belcher, Bronislava Nijinska, David Lichine, and Tatiana Riabouchinska (one of the celebrated "baby ballerinas") were among those who guided the young dancer on her way.

But she had to wait until her school days were over before starting upon a career as a dancer. Once she had received her diploma from the Beverly Hills High School, there was no stopping her, and with Riabouchinska as her friend and chaperon, she set out for the East Coast and the headquarters of professional dance. Serge Denham, director of the Ballet Russe de Monte Carlo, remembered seeing this gifted student and gave her a job in his company. And in 1942, in Canada, she made her formal debut.

For five years, she remained with the Ballet Russe, developing from *corps de ballet* girl to soloist. Balletomanes serving overseas in the Armed Forces during World War II would receive mysterious and enthusiastic communications from friends at home telling of a miraculous new dancer with the peculiar name of Tallchief. No superlatives were spared, and dance-loving soldiers were given an extra reason for wanting to come home, for apparently a new star was shining over the horizon.

The reports were true. A new glitter and a new force were to be found in ballet when Tallchief was on stage as she danced in roles both large and small in *Ballet Imperial, Serenade, Gaité Parisienne, Chopin Concerto, Snow Maiden,* and *Danses Concertantes.* A pagan lustiness marked her Zobeide in *Scheherazade,* and to the role of the Coquette (which she created) in *Night Shadow,* she brought an intensity of action which drew the eye to her characterization.

It was *Le Baiser de la Fée,* however, which gave Tallchief the opportunity to prove that she was more than a superb soloist, that she was a ballerina. Under the direction of George Balanchine (later to become her first husband), she mastered the role of the fairy as, perhaps, no one had ever mastered it before. In the opening scenes she was cool and remote, her fantastic technique disciplined by a style which made her movements seem to be those of a fairy queen for whom the difficult was simple, and in the closing passages she was still remote but very desirable as she led the youth, whose brow she had kissed in distant days, to his enchanted destiny.

Between these two scenes, Tallchief was called upon to present the fairy in the guise of a gypsy. Here was fury and passion and an earthly magic quite different from that of fairyland. She grabbed the hand of the bewildered young man and, circling around him with swift frenzy, read a fate which she pretended to see in his palm. Her hair lashed him, her burning presence hypnotized him. Then, pressing herself close to his back, she pointed with implacable gesture the direction of his future and, as he hesitated, shoved him forward. Again and again this pattern was repeated as the gypsy propelled the boy toward that unknown destiny decreed by a kiss.

Actually, this new American ballerina was born, professionally speaking, in Paris, for it was at the Paris Opéra, as guest artist, that Tallchief not only danced the role of the fairy-gypsy in *Baiser* but also assumed the principal parts in *Serenade* and *Apollo*. This was in the spring of 1947, and in the fall of that year she became ballerina of the new Ballet Society, shortly to emerge as the New York City Ballet.

With the City Ballet, new and fresh and vital, as her company and with Balanchine creating for her unique artistry, it was inevitable that she should grow quickly into one of the great ballerinas of her day. First to be exploited was her prodigious technique, and Balanchine was just the man for that. He would and did ask the seemingly impossible of her, and she responded. Occasionally, she would say unbelievingly, "Oh, George!" but she never refused to try (and ultimately to do faultlessly) a mad mixture of turns involving the quick shift of axis from one foot to another, an off-balance spin, *entrechats-huit*, air-turns landing *sur les pointes*, and almost anything else inside and outside the book of ballet.

Two ballets, one pure dance and the other dramatic but both classical in technique, are closely associated with her. The first is, of course, *Symphony in C*. This is a study in movement development, in imperial style, in theatrical glitter. Her *entrée* is fleet; the

218

multiple turns, each ending in a different direction with arm extended, are sharp yet gracious; the accent is not upon shimmer but upon flash, the flash of a jewel capturing brilliant light in each of its facets. Here is Camargo as she might have appeared in an atomic age, supersonic as opposed to merely fast, steel as distinct from lacquer.

The second ballet is *Firebird*. And here the primitive may truly shine, for this is a bird, wild and free, a creature of air and of fire. Perhaps she is only a dancer spinning with incredible speed around the stage or, with flashing sword, leaping into the midst of heroes and demons, but she seems to be no mere executant of steps. She is, in the eyes of the watchers, an enchanted being skimming the earth, slashing the air with a shining, mercurial body.

The coloratura soprano climbs the scale seeking new heights of excitement, she trills, she holds a note until sound and echo seem to meet; and Tallchief, in dance, can mirror the pyrotechnics of such singing. In *Sylvia: Pas de Deux*, she spins long phrases of action, her leaps and jumps carry her to new planes of adventure, her balances defy the inexorable pull of gravity. The same may be said for her role in the Balanchine-Minkus *Pas de Trois* or in any of a number of other ballets. But what of her acting, what of her tenderness and sensitivity?

Do you remember her as the sweet Eurydice of *Orpheus*, clinging lovingly to the body of the blindfolded Orpheus as he leads her from Hell to Earth? Who can forget her in *Guests* as she touches hands with one who is separated from her by invisible barriers of convention and prejudice? For Tallchief can be as soft as she can be strong, as glowing as she can be flashing. True, her forte seems to lie in physical power used to perfection, but the actress, the purveyor of mood and color, is also present.

219

Naturally, her position as one of the world's top ballerinas would be insecure, or at least arguable, if she had not proffered her conception of the Queen of the Swans. But she has been eminently successful in two versions of the Petipa-Ivanov masterpiece. In the customary one-act version, which she has danced with Ballet Theatre, her style is pure Petipa, her mime exquisite, her virtuosity impeccable. Others have probed deeper into the character of the Queen and revealed more of the emotional conflicts besetting this heroine, but no one has danced its measures of action more brilliantly. The second one-act treatment, choreographed by Balanchine, suits her even better, for the accent is upon movement rather than upon drama, and although she defines clearly the romantic longings and the fears of the Queen, one remembers her mainly as the key figure in mass designs of great beauty as she moves in and out of her army of swan maidens or as a soloist who combines the fluttering speed of a winged creature with the commanding elegance of a queen.

Catherine de Medici, wherever the will of the Almighty may have placed her for her deeds of valor and of evil, must be viewing with surprise and, perhaps, with approval the results of a way of dance she helped to establish. Only amazement could be her reaction to the virtuosity of Tallchief. Celestial (?) gasps would greet the stabbing legs, the vertiginous *pirouettes*, the head-high *battements*, the endless array of technical feats of which Tallchief is capable. But she would understand the erect stance, the graciousness of gesture, the proud and assured bearing, the courtly *grande révérence*. And she would recognize in an American Indian girl the ageless manners of a princess. For Catherine de Medici would see before her, in the person of Maria Tallchief, a star performer, a true "Queen of the Dance."

220

GLOSSARY

Adagio, ah-dah'-jho: A dance in slow tempo, usually associated with that section of a classical *pas de deux* in which the ballerina, assisted by her partner, displays her balance, her line, her mastery of slow and flowing movements.

Allegro, ahl-lay'-gro: A dance in fast tempo.

Arabesque, ar-ah-besk': A traditional pose in which the dancer stands on one leg with the other leg extended in a straight line. The arms also are extended, but their positions may vary.

Ballerina, bal-leh-ree'-nah: A principal female dancer in a ballet company. In a company which has several ballerinas the star is usually classified as the *prima ballerina.* The highest ballerina post—one that is rarely granted—is *prima ballerina assoluta.*

Ballet d'Action, bal-lay' dak-see-ohn': A ballet with a plot.

Balletomane, bal-leh-to-mayn': A ballet fan, one who attends performances faithfully and endeavors to spread interest in the art among friends and acquaintances.

Ballon, bal-lohn': The bouncing quality, the resilience of a dancer demonstrated during leaps, jumps, or any action which carries him into the air.

Battement, bat-mahn': Action of the leg, a kick.

Battu, bat-tu': A step which incorporates a beat of the legs striking together—related to the *cabriole.*

Bourrée, boor-ray': A sixteenth-century court dance. *See also* Pas de bourrée.

BASIC ARABESQUE, UPRIGHT POSITION, IN DARK LINES. ARABESQUE PENCHÉ, OR BENDING FORWARD POSITION, IN DOTTED LINES

Attitude, ah-tee-tuhd': Another traditional pose in which the dancer stands on one leg, but here the other leg, though raised high, is bent at the knee.

THREE VIEWS OF AN ATTITUDE

221

Cabriole, kah-bree-ohl': A spectacular movement (formerly for men primarily) in the air in which the calves of the legs beat together to the front, back, or side. The legs, knees straight, toes pointed, are beaten at an angle from the body and not directly underneath it.

Caractère, kah-rahk-tair': A character dancer, one who performs nonclassical national dances in ballet. In *demi-caractère* the dancer may be required to fuse classic dancing with folk measures or comedy elements.

Chaconne, shah-kohn': An eighteenth-century dance, presumably of Spanish origin.

Coda, ko'-dah: The closing section of a *pas de deux* or ballet.

Corps de Ballet, kor d' bal-lay': The ensemble, the group dancers (nonsoloists) of a ballet company.

Coryphée, ko-ree-fay': A dancer ranked between a *corps de ballet* member and a soloist. One who dances with a small group in passages distinct from those performed by full ensemble. The term applies primarily to a member of the former Russian Imperial Ballet.

Danse D'École, dahns day-kohl': The classic dance. The ballet technique based upon the five positions and the turnout of the limbs.

Danseur Noble, dahn-ser' nobl: Classical male dancer.

Développé, day-vlo-pay': The gradual unfolding to the front, side, or back of the leg as it is raised in an extension.

Elevation: The ability to perform aerial action.

Entrechat, ahn-treh-shah': A movement in which the dancer jumps directly up and crosses his feet several times (*entrechat quatre, entrechat six,* etc.) while in air.

Entrée, ahn-tray': An entrance. The opening section of a *grand pas de deux* or any separate section, performed by a group of dancers in a suite of dances.

The Five Positions: The basic positions of the feet in ballet.

Position One: heels together, feet turned out.

Position Two: heels separated, feet form straight line.

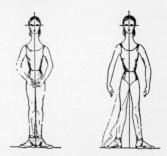

FIRST AND SECOND POSITIONS, DOTTED LINE IS TRANSITION TO THIRD POSITION

DEVELOPPÉ À LA SECONDE

Position Three: heels touching arches of opposite feet, feet turned out.

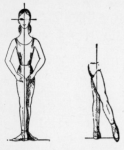

THIRD POSITION AND TRANSITION TO FOURTH POSITION

Position Four: one foot placed in front of other foot but separated, turnout retained.

FOURTH POSITION, SIDE AND FRONT VIEWS

Position Five: the heel of one foot placed against big-toe joint of opposite foot, turnout, as in all positions, maintained.

FIFTH POSITION

Fouetté, fwet-tay': A whipping movement of the leg which propels the dancer into a turn or series of turns while balanced on the other leg.

FOUETTÉ

Gargouillade, gar-gwee-yahd': An aerial step in which the legs, with bent knees at the peak of the leap, are drawn up with the leading foot describing a small outward circle in air and the other foot making a small inward circle.

Gavotte, gah-vaht': An early peasant dance and, in the eighteenth century, a popular court dance.

Gigue, jheeg: A jig, a lively dance particularly popular in the eighteenth century.

Grand Jeté, grahn jheht-tay': A large leap.

GRANDE JETÉ

Loure, loor: A slow and stately dance related to the livelier *gigue.*

Modern Dance: Developed during the twentieth century in America and in Central Europe. A form of dance which, unlike the classic

223

ballet, has no set vocabulary of movement, although it does possess a highly evolved technique for training the body.

Musette, mew-zet′: Pastoral passages familiar to operagoers in the eighteenth century.

Pas de Basque, pah d' bahsk: Literally, Basque step. A smooth, sliding step.

Pas de Bourrée, pah d' boor-ray′: Short, even, usually fast walking steps on ball of foot with the feet kept close together. Mainly done on *pointes* by the female dancer.

Pas de Deux, pas d' der: A dance for two.

Pas de Trois, pas d' twah: A dance for three.

Passepied, pahs-pee-ay′: A lively and gay French court dance.

Pirouette, pih-roo-et′: A turn on one foot.

PIROUETTE I, II

Plié, plee-ay′.

Demi Plié, deh-mee′ plee-ay′ (half bend): A bending of the standing knee, or both knees (with heels on the floor) which enables a dancer to spring from the floor with smoothness. The *plié* is also the landing position after a spring or jump.

Grande Plié, grahnd plee-ay′ (full bend): A deep bending of both knees well turned out from the hip with the body well centered and lowered to a squatting position. Practiced in all five positions as an exercise for balance and control.

Pointe, pwant: The toe.

Sur les Pointes, suhr lay pwant: Indicates that the dancer (female) is dancing on the very tips of her toes.

Sur les Demi-Pointes, suhr lay deh-mee pwant: Indicates that the dancer is dancing high on the ball of the foot.

Port de Bras, por d' brah: Term for the classical position of the arms.

Prima Ballerina, pree′-mah bal-leh-ree′-nah: *See* Ballerina.

Prima Ballerina Assoluta, pree′-mah bal-leh-ree′-nah ah-so-loo′-tah. *See* Ballerina.

Relevé, reh-leh-vay′: The rising upon *pointe* or *demi-pointe* from flat-foot position.

Rigaudon, ree-go-dohn′: A light and joyous court dance.

Sarabande, sah-rah-bahnd′: An ancient court dance of Moorish origin.

Terre-à-Terre, tair-ah-tair: Steps done on the ground, not aerial.

Tights: The skin-tight, stockinglike garment reaching from waist to feet.

Tutu, too-too′: The ballet skirt. In the romantic style it reaches almost to the ankle; in the later classic ballet, it can resemble a big powder puff extending stiffly from the hips and leaving the limbs entirely visible.